The Miracle and Power of Blessing

by

Maurice Berquist

**Illustrations by
Dick Maloney**

**Published by
Warner Press, Inc.
Anderson, Indiana**

To Mother Perry, who first introduced me to the idea of blessing. She not only taught the principle, but blessed everyone she met. Of her fourteen children, eleven are living. Anyone who touches their lives is blessed. They are Clive, Clara, Faye, Clarence, Ollie, Paul, Mable, Coleman, Guy, Eleanor, and Helen Jo.

Contents

Preface

Blessing walked into my life wearing a large, almost over-powering flowered hat. I will never forget the day.

While I was a student in college I was invited to speak to a large international convention. This address was not to be the main one of the evening—it was to be a short introductory talk preceding the main address by veteran missionary statesman E. Stanley Jones.

Many years have passed since that time when I stood trembling before the packed auditorium. I cannot remember one thing that I said, nor can I remember anything that E. Stanley Jones said. I only know that when the speaking was finished the people crowded around Dr. Jones like a swarm of bees. They wanted his autograph, wanted to shake hands with him or ask him a question.

I walked off the stage, feeling as insignificant as I ever have in my whole life. No one had come to talk to me or comment on my brief talk. No one? Almost no one. One little old lady wearing an outrageously flowered hat came to shake my hand. She smiled.

"Bless you, my son," she said. "You gave a wonderful talk. I pray that God will bless your life and make you a blessing to everyone as long as you live. You were a blessing to me today. Bless you, oh bless you."

Then the enormous hat with the little lady under it disappeared in the crowd. The memory of her smile stayed with me.

Later in the evening, I met with some of my college friends. They were curious to know how it felt to share the platform with a world-famous personality.

"It's a little like crawling out from under Plymouth Rock and finding someone standing on top of it," I explained. "But one thing happened that made me feel better—a little old lady in a flowered hat. She came up to me and said, 'Bless you, young man.' Then she heaped a few more blessings on me and walked away. I never did hear her name."

"That has to be 'Mother Perry,' " someone said. "She goes around blessing all kinds of things. One of her favorite expressions is 'Bless the Lord.' "

In the months and years that followed, I learned to appreciate the attitude of this remarkable lady. Though many severe trials came to her, she managed to bless the Lord through all of them. She discovered a strange, almost mystical power over the things that usually defeat and frustrate people. Without explaining how she did it, she managed to put a key in my hands that unlocked many doors. She made me think about the strange power of blessing. She encouraged me to share it with other people.

Even after these years, I am not exactly sure why it works. I am fully persuaded *that* it works, and it works for anyone.

This book has been born out of a desire to share the Good News. Bless you as you read it.

Introduction

She was wonderful. Her name was Sally Erickson and she was really wonderful. But I could not tell her. Her mind was closed against the whole idea. Her dull gray eyes shifted listlessly like hungry sparrows looking for food on a concrete pavement. There was no way I could look into those sad eyes and say, "You are really wonderful."

If beauty was hidden in that heavily lined face I could not see it. Nor could she. Had she looked in a mirror to find some trace of hope, some trace of beauty, her mocking image would have plunged her into deeper despair.

You have seen people like her. Sloping shoulders, shuffling feet, furtively darting eyes—all these make up the picture of someone who has the ability to live with joy but has lost the will to search for it.

Shortly after meeting her I learned that she had reason to be discouraged. Ravaged by sickness, plagued with family problems, her mind was leaving her.

Since the normal way of solving problems was not working for her, she was building a world of fantasy—a world in which she could feel comfortable. It was a world of insanity. The doctor had studied it and his verdict was simple—frightening but simple: "Next Thursday, ma'am, we will send you to Tuscaloosa. Maybe they can get that mind of yours straightened out." The doctor had tried sincerely to help, but he could not. His verdict was another act of despair.

How, then, could I think that this bundle of human misery was wonderful. It is easy to see why I could not say "You are wonderful." To try would be mockery—mockery of the cruelest kind.

How did I meet her? Why do I think she is wonderful? An even more interesting question is to ask why she herself believes that life is wonderful—and that she as a part of it is wonderful. Something came into her thoughts, almost like some kind of reverse thief who left presents instead of taking them. This secretive intruder put a key in her hands that unlocked a whole new world, a world of real physical health and real mental health.

What kind of key? Where is that key? Can any one of us find a key like that that will let us walk into a room full of magic mirrors that will reflect new images of ourselves? Can it be true that these exciting images of the person we would like to become are not magic? They are fantasy. They are fact.

There is a key, It is called *blessing*. What a short word that is! A few years ago that word would have slipped in and out of my mind without causing so much as a faint stir. It was a good gray word, a low-voltage word. Like a well-worn overcoat, it was too good to throw away but no longer stylish or really useful. Now it is different. It is a short fuse to an explosive world. It has become the key to thousands of miracles that I know about.

The word *blessing* became the key to turn in the rusty lock of Sally's life. No one could have been more surprised than she when she saw that hidden within her was a world of health and healing, a world of wonder—a wonderful world.

As I write this, I must tell you that there is a wonderful world waiting for you. Bless you, you really are wonderful. Of course, you have always felt that there must be some sort of secret that *some* people discover and you have wondered why you haven't found it.

It's a little like a group of blindfolded men in Ali-Baba's cave. They run their fingers through piles of rubies and diamonds and imagine that they are pebbles. So they walk out empty handed, poor as when they entered.

Sally and I learned together about the word *bless.* Here's how it happened.

"Can I bring my neighbor to your lecture tomorrow morning?" The soft southern drawl of the charming Alabama woman was so beguiling that I almost told her that it would be all right if she wanted to bring a saber-toothed tiger through the magnolia-lined streets of Huntsville. "Of course you may bring her. Why do you ask?"

"Well, she may disturb you. She is not your ordinary

2

southern housewife looking for a place to drink her second cup of coffee. She has problems."

"Haven't we all," I answered.

"Not like hers," she replied. "Physically she is a wreck, a basket case. But worse than that, she is under treatment for a mental illness. Next week she is scheduled to be sent to Tuscaloosa."

"Tuscaloosa?" I asked.

She replied, "That is the state mental hospital."

"If she is that sick," I suggested, "she probably needs some of the things we are talking about. After all, the Church is not a display case for perfect people, but a hospital for sick ones."

"What if she disturbs the meeting?" asked the woman.

"Let's take that chance," I said.

During the lecture the next day I was not sure I had made the right response. The troubled woman was there. So were her troubles. Although I had not been introduced to her, it was not difficult to recognize her.

She found a seat. It did not seem to satisfy her. She found another. Through the hour she was up and down, in and out. It was as though she was being pursued by an enemy that none of us could see.

Frankly it irritated me. It didn't anger me; it just irritated me. But in a sense I welcome irritation. Irritation keeps you alert. It keeps you from settling down too long in one spot. For a speaker, it forces him or her to find new approaches, new insights. Who knows, if people get enough sand in their shell they may, like the oyster, make a pearl. Without the challenge of irritation it is possible to answer questions eloquently that no one is asking, to invent cures for diseases that no one has.

At the close of the lecture I was introduced to the visitor.

"It's nice to meet you, Sally," I said.

"Sally," my soft-voiced friend said, "this is Doctor Berquist."

"Doctor Berquist, I am a sick woman, real sick," the woman responded.

3

"Would you like to have me pray for you," I suggested.

"Why not?" she said.

We walked together to a small room adjoining the auditorium. We walked slowly because I was trying to think of some way I could help. Silently I prayed for guidance. The medical and psychiatric doctors were not the only ones frustrated by her problem. I was frustrated, too.

I asked Sally to be seated in the chair across from me. "Now I am going to pray for you," I said. "Then I want you to pray."

"I don't know how to pray," she replied.

"Don't worry about that," I said reassuringly. "I will pray first and then I will tell you how to pray."

With that introduction I bowed my head, closed my eyes, and began to repeat slowly the words of an ancient Hebrew psalm. I heard myself softly saying the words from that storehouse of songs forged from the flinty hills of trouble.

> Bless the Lord, O my soul:
> and all that is within me, bless his holy name.
> Bless the Lord, O my soul,
> and forget not all his benefits;
> Who forgiveth all thine iniquities;
> Who healeth all thy diseases;
> Who redeemeth thy life from destruction;
> Who crowneth thee with lovingkindness and
> tender mercies.
> Who satisfieth thy mouth with good things;
> So that thy youth is renewed like the eagle's.

A strange quietness filled the little room. I felt impressed to repeat the ancient poem that is recorded in the Old Testament of the Bible by the musician king, David, in Psalm 103:1-6.

I repeated these words more slowly. It was almost as though they were being written on the walls of my mind by some mystic hand. The stillness in the room seemed even deeper and more intense.

4

"Now I want you to repeat these words with me," I said.

Phrase by phrase we spoke the words of this three-thousand-year-old song. Some of the words were spoken falteringly as Sally struggled to form them. But they were spoken. And we did it together.

I cannot forget the moment. Two people, literally strangers, said words together—words that linked them for a moment to infinity. Phrase by phrase Sally's hesitating voice joined mine. "Bless the Lord . . . bless his holy name . . . who forgiveth . . . who healeth all they diseases . . . who redeemeth . . . who crowneth . . . who satisfieth . . . who reneweth."

The words were spoken timidly, almost fearfully, but they were spoken.

During this time my eyes were closed. When I opened them, I looked on a changed face, a surprised face, an almost jubilant face. The ashen look of despair was gone. Sally was changed. The smile on her face was one of astonishment rather than gratitude.

"I feel different," she said joyfully. "Something happened to me."

"Tell me about it," I said.

"I can't tell you because I don't know what happened," she replied. "I simply felt something go through me like electricity and I feel well. I am not sick anymore."

"I believe the Lord has healed you," I told her.

"I can't understand it, but I feel like a different person," she said.

It was true. Something almost unbelievable had happened. The woman was healed. She was not hospitalized. She did not need to be. Both the desperate mental illness and the physical sickness were gone.

Of course, I was delighted. But I was almost as astonished as Sally. As soon as I said good-bye and God bless you I found a place where I could think about what had happened.

What did I do? What did God do? More important, why did God do what he did when I did what I did?

If I could answer these questions I might make one of the

5

most important discoveries of my life. As a matter of fact, I could hardly call it a discovery; I wasn't looking for anything.

I had simply stumbled over a new idea.

Somewhere in the back of my mind is a quotation: "Occasionally he stumbled across a new truth, but he always picked himself up and hurried on as though nothing had happened." I didn't want to be like that.

Something had happened. But what? A heap of encrusted ideas about prayer were shattered. Isn't prayer asking for things? I hadn't asked. Isn't prayer an energetic recounting of our problems in the presence of the Almighty? I had not told God about the agonizing needs that paralyzed Sally's life. Much as I believe in it, I had not "anointed with oil" as the New Testament writer James commands (James 5:14-15). Yet healing had come.

To those who believe, no explanation is necessary. To those who do not believe, no explanation is possible. But I wanted an explanation. Is there some kind of magic in repeating the words of this particular ancient psalm? Had I stumbled across something new? I couldn't hurry on as though nothing had happened. It had happened. My mind bristled with questions—no answers, just questions.

Chapter 1

It Is Not Magic after All

Somewhere in my brain I have a little garden spot where I plant ideas. These ideas, like seeds, lie there for a while and then when things are just right they begin to sprout and grow. Sometimes they grow into worthless weeds and I throw them out. Sometimes they grow into jack-in-the-beanstalk plants, big as trees. They threaten to crowd everything else out of my mind. Sometimes they grow into beautiful concepts that seem to have no useful function. They simply make me feel good.

The seed of blessing was more like an acorn than a radish seed. When it was dropped into my think garden it became a giant tree. It would not be ignored.

When did I first hear the word *blessing*? I believe I first heard it when I was a small child in Kansas. My parents taught us to repeat a prayer that became our routine table grace.

>   Gode Gud,
>   Velsigne maten
>   I Jesus nam,
>   Amen.

The words *Velsigne maten* simply mean "Bless the food." I must have hurried through that prayer a thousand times as I waited impatiently to eat.

The idea of blessing had other roots.

Sometimes when people sneezed somebody else said, *"Gezundheit."* At first I thought that word just sounded a lot like a sneeze and so it was a kind of fighting back. Later

I learned the reason for it. *Gezundheit* is a German word meaning "good health." The origin of the custom is in the idea that sneezing is a way of expelling the bad spirits out of the body, so naturally it was proper to wish that person good health.

Then, of course, there was the shelfful of self-help books I had read. Each book in its own way seemed to say that there is a positive force in the world—a helping, healing power. If anyone could tune in to it, he or she could succeed. It wasn't really a matter of self-help but a matter of tuning in to a power outside one's self.

As these seeds—which I have named "the magic of blessing"—grew in the stubborn soil of my Swedish mind, they were fed by a thousand memories. I remembered the good-luck signs in China. I remembered the hexes and voodoo charms of primitive people. I remembered the mountains of blessing and cursing in Israel.

Could it be that blessing is one of the hidden forces of the universe? Like gravitation, is it a universal law? Of course, gravitation had been working a long time before Sir Isaac Newton saw an apple fall from a tree. He simply put into words what had always been true.

Could an apple fall for me? And could I be able to put the idea into words that would let people believe? It was a terrifying thought—tantalizing but terrifying.

What if I merely made people believe that there were either good or bad forces in the world that are beyond our control? Or even worse, what if these powerful forces were left to the whim of a moody creator? What if the magic of blessing was understood to be black magic, a sinister force?

If anything like these things were true, I should remain silent. Of course, the other possibility is that God doesn't intend for us to learn the secret of the universe. Could it be as Buckminster Fuller says, "The universe is a locked safe with the combination on the inside"?

That wouldn't explain Mother Perry and her thirteen children. It wouldn't explain the 330-pound lady who discovered the way to bless herself into a size-twelve dress. Or it wouldn't explain Don and Maxine McCall, who managed to change a cranky fellow teacher into an absolute charmer. And what about Nancy and her wonderful pumpkin and Ray and his poinsettia? If this is not a workable idea these people are going to have to find some kind of explanation. Their stories will follow later, but first let me tell you how the nagging scientific side of my brain was satisfied. I discovered the Parallel Principle.

Chapter 2

Sinai May Not Be So Far from DeLand, Florida

My time came for jury duty in DeLand, Florida. DeLand is the home of prestigious Stetson University where budding lawyers are trained. Maybe the law of blessing would find a home here. DeLand is not a mountain by any stretch of imagination; it is flat as bride's biscuits. But it might turn out to be my own personal mount of blessing. Here are the facts.

Jury duty is not all that exciting. Morning dragged wearily along and any new thought would have been as welcome as payday. A break for lunch was announced. At that point it sounded exciting.

One of the jurors and I drove to the edge of town to find a restaurant. Perhaps because the long morning with its tiring legalities had forced us to be silent, Jim, my new friend, seemed overly talkative.

"Do you see those power lines that run along the highway?" he asked.

This was scarcely a scientific discovery to compare with the law of gravity. But it was conversation. I joined in. "Yes, I see the wires. They look like all the other wires that stretch across the country."

My friend continued, "Everyone knows that these wires carry electricity. Right?"

"Right," I responded.

"But do you know that you can get electricity from these wires without actually being connected to them?" he asked.

"No. How?" I said.

"Well it is like this," he explained. "If you pull a copper wire parallel to these overhead wires you get a transfer of power. Even though the second wire is not touching the overhead wires, even though it is not connected to anything like a generator or dynamo, power will come into it. Just as soon as it gets parallel, power will come."

"Really?" I responded skeptically.

Frankly it sounded impossible to me; but impossible or not, it was an intriguing idea.

A few moments later we parked our car in front of the most likely looking restaurant we could find. Inside we found a table, a menu, and the usual sarcophagus-shaped napkin holder. I do not remember what I ordered. It was in fact quite mediocre, and quite forgettable.

I do remember taking a napkin from its holder and drawing on it. I sketched the power lines and the supporting poles. The blaring jukebox added very little to my primitive art.

I smiled at my effort. It would not take any prize, I am sure, but it did look like the power lines we had seen. The bird I sketched looked strangely like a high-flying turtle, but that did not seem too important.

Now comes the important part, I thought. It isn't news that in these copper wires flows the power to do the work of the world. Cities are lit, toast is made, television sets blare, washing machines go through their antics—all with the power of electricity. The important thing is to get connected in some firm, visible way with these power lines.

Now comes the incredible part, I thought as I reached for another napkin. Could a wire that was not connected to these power lines draw power from them? Simply by making the wire parallel, would I be able to receive power?

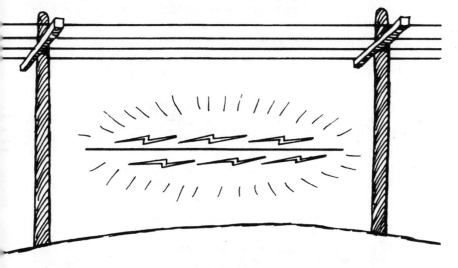

I drew another set of poles and wires. I had done it. Of course it was only an illustration hastily drawn on a restaurant napkin. The second drawing was just like the first with one exception, well actually two exceptions.

I abandoned the idea of the bird on the wire. Frivolity seemed out of place at that moment. More important, I had added a second line—the parallel line. It was charged with electricity. Maybe this was the elusive law of blessing I was looking for.

Thoughts of Benjamin Franklin floated in my mind. Naturally I didn't know Mr. Franklin personally, but I had seen pictures of him with his kite. He had the feeling that there was electrical power above him. Sending a kite up into the storm clouds connected him with this power. If I may be allowed a jest, what had simply been an idea to him became a shocking reality. He was in touch with a power he could not understand. Neither could he ignore it.

I thought of this as I sat in the humble restaurant in DeLand. I seemed to be in a holy place. The blaring jukebox might well have been a cathedral organ.

Could this simple illustration be the answer to my question: How do I make the power of the universe work for me? Could it explain why certain people always seem to be charged with energy and success?

The idea seemed so simple that it was almost unbelievable. On the other hand, it seemed so simple that it must be true. If indeed God is a God of blessing, the source of goodness for all people, would he not be the *ultimate power*?

By whatever name God is called, his power, silent as electricity in the overhead wires, spans the world. It can do anything.

The problem is that we cannot reach up with our bare hands and take hold of God. That does not mean that he cannot reach us.

People obviously reach out toward whatever god they believe controls the world. This experience is called prayer. Prayer in some form is found all over the earth.

In spite of people's fervent prayers, they are still needy. Is it because God doesn't care or that he is not able to help them? Obviously not. It is simply that they have not understood how to pray. Prayer is not overcoming the reluctance of an unwilling God. Instead, prayer is laying hold of the willingness of God.

Could prayer be the movement of the human mind that makes it parallel with God's nature, God's plan? Simply

14

lining one's thoughts so that they flow in the direction of God's thoughts might be the answer.

Since God is a blesser, we must become blessers. The psalm instructs us, "Bless the Lord." This is a strange request. But since there is no doubt that God constantly blesses people, that is the direction in which his mind flows. We must make our minds flow the same way. When that happens and we parallel the thoughts of God, his power comes to us.

Why did the disciples of Jesus cry out, "Lord, teach us to pray"? Obviously they knew they were missing something.

What was Jesus' answer? What was—and is—the magic formula? Jesus said, "This is the way you should pray." Then he gave what is called the Lord's Prayer. Does it fit these new ideas of the magic of blessing? Let us look at it.

"Our Father which art in heaven." Can this relate to our overhead wires, evidence of another world?

"Hallowed be thy name." That fits. If we believe in any kind of God at all, we believe in his power. And we are awed by it. Trying to explain power like that would be like bringing a bottleful of water home from Niagara Falls to explain to the family what Niagara Falls really is.

Not long ago as I flew to Arizona I saw from the sky an electrical storm. Lightning flashed in majestic arcs through the darkened sky. Within those flashes was power enough to light an entire city. God was simply getting ready to water our radishes.

God has that kind of power. Lightning doesn't explain it, however. His is power with a purpose, power with a reason. He couldn't and wouldn't do anything inconsistent with his nature, with his name. No wonder there is a sense of awe. No wonder we say, "hallowed be thy name." Power and love like that deserve respect.

What comes next in the Lord's Prayer? Oh yes, "Thy kingdom come. Thy will be done in earth, as it is in heaven."

The whole idea of God's kingdom has intrigued me for a long time. I have trouble with the idea of the King of the Universe parading down Main Street on a white horse.

What kind of crown will we fashion for him who holds constellations of stars in his hand?

Does Jesus' prayer help us understand the Kingdom? Perhaps the Parallel Principle helps us. For God to get done what he wants to get done—and since he is a king with a kingdom, why not?—he needs people to line up with his will and his character. Where? On the earth, obviously.

While electricity certainly doesn't explain God, it may illustrate something of his nature. He has power. Impartiality is also his. He is invisible, too.

In the same way that the overhead power lines provide us with the ability to do all the things we need done, God's power is always there. Whether or not you receive the things you need, healing, for example, depends not so much upon what God chooses to do for you as it does upon you. Small wonder that we need to pray.

Since God cannot change, we must. *"Jesus Christ the same yesterday, and today, and forever"* (Heb. 13:8). The Apostle Paul must have known this principle well. He wrote, "Blessed be the God and Father of our Lord Jesus Christ, who has blessed us in Christ with every spiritual blessing in the *heavenly places"* (Eph. 1:3, italic for emphasis).

What a revelation! Questions that had plagued me for years were suddenly finding answers. It always seemed a little foolish to believe in a God of love who would withhold good things from people just because they didn't cry loudly enough. Or maybe he would hang on to the blessings he had promised until the situation became desperate, or maybe until the person had learned how to say the right words in the right language.

That didn't make sense. But the problem remained. Any intelligent skeptic could ask it: "If God answers all prayers (as the Bible certainly promises), would God answer requests for things that would be bad for us?"

Certainly not. What human father would give his four-year-old child a sharp razor for a toy? Would the child's crying change the father's mind? Would the child get the razor simply by kneeling while he or she asked? Or by standing? Or by lifting his or her hands toward the ceiling? If the child cried long enough, would the father relent with a resounding and destructive yes?

What about God? Will he? Obviously God doesn't answer every whining request with a thundering yes.

Didn't Jesus say, "Whatsoever things you ask in my name believing, you will receive of my Father in heaven"? Of course he did. And that promise is like a vault full of treasures. It is not like Buckminster Fuller's locked safe with the combination on the inside. The combination is printed on the door. The key is not hidden. Ask in my name, he said.

If our mind is thinking like the mind of Jesus, it would seem natural that we would ask for the kinds of things that would not be an embarrassment to his name. In some sort of mystical way, would not the request and the answer be a part of the work of Jesus—just as though he were here in person?

I have no idea how a volcano feels just before it erupts, but I felt some kind of cosmic excitement as I began to let one idea light the fuse of another, like a string of fire-crackers.

Two problems remained. First, is the illustration of the electrical wires actually true? Then, does the Bible in its total message support these explosive ideas? I began a long search to find out for myself.

Infinite Power

About the time I was searching for ways to make the Parallel Principle make sense to people, I was involved in helping to build a school and church complex. We were looking for helping hands and soon discovered that they were located at the end of our arms.

So we worked. Men of the church gave up most of their free time for a year to help build. Women worked, too. Sometimes they worked with pots and pans to feed the hungry crew. Sometimes they abandoned the traditionally sexist roles and took up hammers, saws, and brushes.

One day I worked with Frank Hogan. There are two things you need to know about Frank Hogan. First of all, Frank is a weight lifter. He is a muscular giant. He has muscles in all of the places that men usually have muscles; he also has muscles in places where I don't even have places to put them. He would be embarrassed to find himself described by a poet, but I can't resist comparing him with the blacksmith Henry Wadsworth Longfellow wrote about:

> The smith a mighty man is he
> With large and sinewy hands;
> The muscles in his brawny arms
> Are strong as iron bands.

Frank is like that; he is gentle. Gentle or not, however, with a physique like that who is going to doubt his opinion?

To earn his living Frank works for the Florida Power and Light Company. He installs electrical lines. He is familiar with working around the thousands of volts that scurry along these copper highways. He is respectful of them as well. That is the reason he is still alive to flex his muscles.

As we worked I asked him, "Frank, I heard something the other day that is so amazing I can't forget it. I find it hard to believe. I heard that if you pull a copper wire parallel to the overhead wires that carry electricity, even though the second wire is not connected to anything, power will come to it. It will become charged with electricity. Is that true?"

"Certainly," he replied.

"Well, if it is true," I continued, "I want to be absolutely, I mean *absolutely,* sure. If it is true it is an illustration of how spiritual power works. It may be revolutionary. Since it is so exciting I am bound to talk about it.

"Now can you imagine me in front of a group of people. I am describing this phenomenon and making the spiritual application. When the lecture is over I discover that the people are electrical engineers. I would hate to be wrong."

Frank understood. So he patiently explained to me what really happens.

"This principle is one of the first things we are taught when we start to work installing power lines," he said. "If there are active power lines above the place where we are working we have to take special care. If we accidentally get a piece of wire in parallel with these lines it can pick up electricity from the overhead lines. Unless we ground that wire, it can develop enough of an electrical charge to kill a person.

What an exciting idea! It's a trifle frightening, but it is exciting, too.

If we assume that there is an infinite power above us, what would keep that power from working inside us? If there is power to heal, why are we ever sick? If there is a power to forgive, why do we feel guilty? If there is a power to renew our youth, why do we get old? The idea of an all-powerful God is certainly not new. But if all that power and willingness are somewhere above us, what keeps it from working in us? Nothing. Nothing can keep it from invading our lives (and revolutionizing them) except ourselves. We are not parallel to the purpose and plan of that infinite power. In other words, we are negative while God is positive.

With the electrical illustration it is that simple. When the two wires are running the same direction, power is transferred. When they are at right angles to each other, nothing happens.

Prayer, then, becomes the process by which we line our minds up with the mind of God. Even though we may not understand what is happening, something happens.

Could that be the reason Sally Erickson in Alabama was instantly healed? She simply repeated those words of blessing. Can words make that much difference?

They can. Later we will explain how words—simple words—become the pilot of your life, the guide of your destiny. If you can control your world, you can control your life.

Learn to bless.

Chapter 3

What Does It Mean to Bless?

Most people don't read complete sentences. They read the first part and guess the second part. I'm guilty of that. In the case of Psalm 103, I am a horrible example. I read "Bless the Lord," but my mind is saying, "Lord, bless me."

The problem is that I want to pour a fresh idea into a mind already corrupted with an accumulation of miscella-

neous ideas I have picked up from my training. If anyone would ask me what to label this hodgepodge of information, I would have to say with a fair amount of pride, "This is my understanding of the Bible." Misunderstanding would have been more like it.

It's not impossible to put a new idea into a forty-year-old mind. Difficult, yes. But not impossible.

Our minds resemble buckets of paint. Let's imagine a conversation between you and me. I dip into my mental tank and pull up a bucket of yellow paint which I am going to pour into your mind. Your mind, however, is not empty. It is full of blue paint. What happens when my message reaches your mind? You will hear green. That is what happens when yellow and blue paint are mixed. A lot of time will pass before you really start hearing what I am saying.

That may explain why I had to read Psalm 103 so many times before I finally realized that it said I was to bless the Lord, not to ask the Lord to bless me.

Even more than this, I had to search for a new meaning to this superpowerful word. Is it the same as *praise*? Is it magic? If so, how are you going to perform sleight of hand with the Almighty?

If there really is a treasure chest filled with forgiveness, healing, redemption, renewal, and abundance, I needed to unlock it. And if blessing is the key, I needed to discover how to use it.

I turned to the Bible itself. An old Latin phrase spoken to me by Kenneth Scott Foreman flashed across my mind: *Scriptura Scripturae Interpres* ("Scripture by scripture is interpreted").

Within the Bible itself I find illustrations of people who took hold of the handle of blessing as a lever to move the world. In the Old Testament Isaac blessed Jacob. The story is told in Genesis 27. The simple narrative is that while Isaac was growing older he knew that he had to give a special gift to his older son. This was called a birthright. It had nothing to do with the goodness or badness of the son; it was simply his because he managed an earlier arrival than his other brothers. Without Isaac's knowledge, however, Esau, the older son, had traded his birthright to Jacob for a meal.

The incident was forgotten until that important day when the aged Isaac called his son Esau. He said, "Behold now, I am old, I know not the day of my death. Now therefore take, I pray thee, thy weapons, thy quiver and thy bow, and go out to the field, and take me some venison; And make me a savory meat, such as I love, and bring it to me, that I may eat; that my soul may bless thee before I die" (vv. 2-4).

Rebekah, Isaac's wife, overheard this conversation. She conspired with the younger son, Jacob, to trick Isaac into giving him the blessing. She made the stew, disguised Jacob, and sent him into the old man.

"And Isaac said unto Jacob, Come near, I pray thee, that I may feel thee, my son, whether thou be my very son Esau or not. And Jacob went near unto Isaac his father; and he felt him, and said, The voice is Jacob's voice, but the hands are the hands of Esau. And he discerned him not . . . so he blessed him" (vv. 21-23).

What was the blessing? Let me repeat it here: "See, the smell of my son is as the smell of a field which the Lord hath blessed: Therefore God give thee of the dew of heaven, and the fatness of the earth, and plenty of corn and wine: Let people serve thee . . . be lord over thy brethren, and let thy mother's sons bow down to thee: cursed be every one that curseth thee, and blessed be he that blesseth thee" (vv. 27-29).

When this was finished, Esau came in from the field. He assumed that his father would be waiting with the blessing, but he was too late. Isaac realized he had been deceived. Esau was bitter. A mistake had been made. But there was no turning back.

Trying to recover what he could from his brother's trickery, Esau said, "Hast thou but one blessing, my father? Bless me."

Isaac did bless him, but not with the same blessing he had given his younger brother. He had to give another. "Behold, thy dwelling shall be in the fatness of the earth, and of the dew of heaven from above; And by thy sword shalt thou live, and shalt serve thy brother; and it shall come to pass when thou shalt have the dominion, that thou shalt break his yoke from off thy neck" (vv. 39-40).

Whether or not I like the story, some interesting things come out of it.

1. Blessing is highly desirable; it actually gives something.

2. The person receiving it does not need to be worthy of it. Obviously Jacob had lied and been deceptive and greedy, but he got the best blessing.

3. A blessing is conferred, given, bestowed. It apparently cannot be taken back.

4. The word *bless* is not to be confused with the word *praise*. For the moment I want you to compare the two as they might appear in this story.

There is no way that Isaac could feel like praising Jacob. In fact, if we were able to show some home movies of the Jacob-Esau scene, we would probably see that this trickster Jacob was always getting away with something. Esau, the plodding, earthy, hard-working son did all the work and Jacob got the credit. Even though Isaac's eyes were dim, he must have discerned that something was wrong. Certainly he would not praise Jacob for this.

As we venture a little farther into the magic land of blessing, we will see that the people who need blessing the most are the ones who deserve it the least. We cannot wait until they are worthy of praise before we bless them. God acts like that.

Jacob got the blessing and Esau had to be satisfied with a substitute blessing.

Chapter 4

A Short Course in Cursing and Blessing

Sometimes the best way to explain a word is to tell what it is not. For example, white is the opposite of black; light is the opposite of darkness. Yes is the opposite of no. Cursing is the opposite of blessing.

It is not likely that anyone reading this far will feel guilty about cursing. "Nice people don't do it," they say.

Cursing persists. No place in the world, no matter how primitive or sophisticated it may be, is without its forms of cursing and blessing. Voodoo charms and hexes, curses and incantations all bring evil down upon people. Blessings and benedictions, rituals and ceremonies all try to place some positive force in action. It is so all over the world.

Do nice people curse? It's possible. *Darling* isn't always a nice word. I have met women who could nail their husband to the wall with the lilting word, *Darling*. Let's imagine how it can happen.

Let's create a scene like this. We are seated around the friendly table of a hospitable family. Conversation has drifted around to the subject of fishing. At this the husband proudly relates his prize fishing story.

"We were fishing in Kentucky Lake. I started to reel my line in and thought that I must have snagged the bottom of the lake. Then I knew I had a fish, a big one, the granddaddy of them all. For thirty minutes I fought that fish. When I finally pulled him into the boat, he was *that* long."

"Darling." The wife has spoken.

The air chills. The smiling fisherman wilts like yesterday's soufflé. Color drains from his face.

You steal a glance at his wife and discover where the color has gone. Veins in her neck begin to stand out; her eyes narrow. War is on.

With a little luck you manage to change the conversation. The subject of fishing leaves the candle-lit battlefield. Subjects like politics or religion seem safer. Finally you and the other guests leave.

Now let us look back on the honeymoon cottage. Let us listen to the conversation.

"You certainly cut me down tonight, Hortense."

"What did I say?"

"It's not what you said; it's what you meant."

"What did I say?"

"You said 'darling.' "

"Darling. All I can say, Henry, is that you must be getting pretty thin-skinned if I can't call you darling in front of a few friends."

At this point I would like to leave the imagined conversation. In fact, I would like to have left it a long time ago. However, it does make something pretty obvious. It doesn't really matter what precise words you use. Negative attitudes can leak out of almost any sugar-coated word in the dictionary, *darling* included.

A shocking fact comes to light. All forms of negative talking are some form of cursing. They certainly do not bless. Flowers will wilt under such a barrage. People have their natural milk of human kindness curdled by such talk.

A broad treatment for all such talk comes from the Apostle Paul: "Bless and curse not."

How Do You Start to Bless Something?

Christopher Morley said, "No man has enough bees in his own bonnet to pollinate the flowers of his own mind. Import me a few strange notions."

Since your mind is the place where all these exciting miracles are going to take place, I should let you know my strategy. Whether or not you accept the commands of the Bible about blessing, I want to import a few strange, bizarre, and almost incredible stories into your thinking. You do not have to believe them, but you won't be able to forget them.

If you want to know if these stories are really true (They all are. In a few places I have disguised the names and places so that I will not embarrass anyone), simply think about the events. Then try the magic of blessing. Discover that it works for anyone who will use it. Then you will have your own stories; they will undoubtedly be more remarkable than mine.

Honestly, I have scaled down most of my stories because I want to pollinate your mind. I don't want to do more than mildly upset you.

How do you start? When you enroll in the school of blessing, you find out there are three grades. First, learn to bless God. Second, learn to bless yourself. Third, learn to bless other people and then learn to bless situations and things.

The order is important. There seems to be no way to skip grades in God's school of blessing. Whether you are a confirmed churchgoer or a casual reader whose religion consists in vague memory of which church you stay away from, the course is the same. In a day of six-day diets and instant twelve-course Chinese dinners, this may come as a disappointment.

Actually the first-grade courses in the school of blessing are so exciting you will be tempted to stay in grade one. Resist the temptation.

The important thing is to start. Since there is no better time than now, let me give you a turtle-paced technique.

Marcie Espey taught me a lesson before she went to school. Marcie and the little neighbor girl were playing in the front yard of the Florida parsonage. As I approached, Marcie introduced me to her friend.

"Stephanie, this is Mr. Berquist."

"Hi, Stephanie," I answered. Then I paused to think of something else to talk about. Adults are not too good at this sort of thing, I discovered. "How old are you, Stephanie?"

The energetic little brunette on the tricycle said, "I'm three."

Golden-haired Marcie responded, "I'm five."

I had no intention of entering a battle of age consciousness with the two beautiful girls. I was willing to retreat. The girls were not.

Stephanie was not put down by the superior attitude of Marcie. "Well, one of these days I am going to be five, too."

Marcie answered (rather haughtily I thought) "You gotta be four before you can be five."

There is wisdom in that. There are no grades you can skip in God's school.

The Magic of Blessing

As we plod along these strange pathways we may not move fast enough for the "theological hares" who like to speed to conclusions as soon as they read the chapter title. If you are in that class, feel free to skip to the last part of this book. You will find enough theological and biblical profundity to make you stay awake long past the eleven o'clock news. Pace yourself.

Feel free to dip into this account anywhere, move forward or backward. I have put some ideas on the top shelf for intellectual giraffes. Most of the good ideas are put down where I found them in the common experiences of run-of-the-mill people.

This is the plodding turtle-view of the path of blessing. Whenever you feel like sticking your neck out you can make a little progress. If you feel uncertain, simply pull your neck back in and think about things. I do that myself.

Ray was a reluctant convert to the idea of blessing. I don't mean that Ray was slow to understand. He is probably as close to being a genius as anyone we could afford to hire at the church I pastored. I stood in awe of his ability to grasp new ideas—every idea, that is, except the idea of blessing things. He was too slow for even the turtle-paced.

One Wednesday night I talked about the experiment made by Dr. Parker of Redlands University in California. Dr. Parker wanted to find out if there was a way to prove the value of prayer scientifically. The experiment is described in his book *Prayer Can Change Your Life*.

Two identical beds of seeds were planted. The soil was the same in both beds. The care was the same. The only difference was that the students were assigned to bless one bed of seeds and to curse the other.

To the one bed of seeds they would speak encouragingly. "What wonderful seeds you are, and what a tremendous future you will have as you come to flower and blossom." Confidence, even love, was expressed.

To the other group of seeds only negative ideas were spoken. "You wretched seeds. You will never amount to anything; you will never blossom. You will not make it."

31

Soon the results were apparent. The "blessed" seeds germinated early and produced healthy plants. They blossomed early, just as though they were trying desperately to make the nice things spoken about them come true.

Not so for the negatively treated seeds. Most did not sprout at all. Those that did brought forth spindly, sickly plants.

From this experiment I concluded that if plants could respond to loving care, certainly people would. If cursing is bad for flowers, it must be deadly for people. I encouraged my listeners to be positive—to bless people.

Ray was not impressed. That is putting it mildly.

"Most of the time you make sense to me, pastor, but tonight I have to laugh at you. Do you think I am going to believe that seeds in the ground are going to listen to what people say about them. It's not easy to get people to listen to you. Plants never would."

I replied, "I'm just reporting the facts, Ray. I believe it."

That ended it.

It didn't really end it because after a few months Ray came into my office wearing a strange smile on his face. He said, "I want you to come outside and see a poinsettia."

"I have seen a poinsettia," I answered. They grow profusely in Florida.

"You haven't seen this poinsettia," Ray replied.

I was growing impatient. "A poinsettia is a poinsettia," I said.

Ray persisted, "This one is different. Last Christmas George and Margie Van Ness gave Margaret and me a poinsettia. It bloomed during December and January and by February the leaves began falling off. Finally there was nothing left but a bare stalk. We put the clay pot out on the back steps of our house because we didn't know what else to do with it.

"Then one day we thought that George and Margie might come by the house, see our abandoned flower, and think that we didn't appreciate it. So I planted it. By this time there was just a stub of a stalk about the size of a pencil on the verge of being thrown away. I planted it between the main building and the fellowship hall.

"Then," Ray continued, "do you remember that crazy story you told about people talking to seeds and flowers? I laughed at you. But one day I decided to see if it really would work. So each morning for the past couple of months I have walked by this poinsettia as I came to work. I usually carry a glass of iced tea. That's my breakfast. By the time I reached the poinsettia the glass would be nearly empty. I had been throwing the remaining ice cubes to the flower and saying a few words to it."

"What did you say?" I asked.

"I don't remember exactly," Ray replied, "but I would talk to it and say, 'have a nice day,' or 'you're looking good.' Things like that."

"Ray, let me see this poinsettia," I said.

What a demonstration it was. If I had ever been tempted to doubt the jack-and-the-beanstalk story, it would be difficult after this. The pencil-thin stalk of the Christmas poinsettia had grown until it was a bush fully six feet in diameter. It was covered with buds.

A week later Ray came into my office carrying a poinsettia blossom. Even in the peanut butter jar it looked regal. The blossom measured twelve inches across. It was a double blossom. I went out to look at the bush again. Every blossom on it was double.

I was almost speechless. Not quite, however. "That just goes to show what happens when people practice what I preach," I said to Ray.

I decided to practice the blessing principle myself even more fervently than I had done.

This amazing story has another chapter, a sad one. I may as well tell it here.

As this amazing poinsettia continued to grow and blossom I began to tell its story as I lectured. Soon people coming from far and near asked to see the poinsettia. Sometimes they questioned me, "Do you really have a poinsettia like you described or did you just tell the story?"

"Come and see," I replied.

In a world where superlatives are carelessly used to describe mediocrity I guess I can't blame people for being skeptical. On the other hand, a superlative shouldn't masquerade as mediocrity, not even a modest superlative.

The poinsettia never disappointed anyone. In fact, as people came and bragged about the amazing bush it seemed to listen. I noticed one day that it had started bearing triple blossoms.

The story didn't end there. It has a sad chapter. Truth, you know, is a two-edged sword. It cuts two ways. It is great if you use it right and it is destructive if you use it wrong. In the case of the poinsettia something went wrong.

Even a miracle seems commonplace after you have lived around it for a while. As time went on I didn't pay much attention to our famous poinsettia.

One day I glanced at it and was surprised to see that it was shriveling and about to die. That would have been a tragedy. Like a dowdy queen abandoned by her subjects, the lovely flower seemed forlorn and forgotten. But why? Was the blessing principle just a short-term program? What had changed? Then I remembered.

34

Since the days of the first fantastic blossoms we had started a school. The church buildings were crowded with the students of Warner Academy. Students from kindergarten through high school stood in long lines to enter the dining hall. They walked by the poinsettia—they didn't touch or trample it. What did they do? As they walked by the poinsettia they talked about the cafeteria. They talked about the food.

In the event that you have not been in a school cafeteria recently you may not know the code of the road. Every student takes a silent pledge to complain about the food and the service. It is true from Maine to California, from the kindergarten to the university.

We thought perhaps they didn't like our choice of food. We let them choose their own. They complained about that.

"Pizza again. Ugh." Or, "Hamburgers, ugh," they said.

It was almost a ritual. I can't explain it. It is simply a fact of life. None of the students used profane language—our behavior code would not allow that. Sanctified complaining was almost as much a part of student life as homework.

The flower was dying. There had to be a stop to it. "Even if you don't like the food, students, say something nice to the poinsettia. It is not the cook," we pleaded. They must have listened because the flower took a turn for the better.

Erma Bombeck's Rule of Medicine states, "Never go to a doctor whose office plants have died."

My purpose is simple. I want to turn your conversation into a pattern of blessing. However many negative things there are surrounding you, there is a positive power to cope with them.

Although the first chapter of the Gospel of John means more than this sentence will imply, "in the beginning was the word." Words bless or words wilt.

Chapter 5

What Happens When You Enter the Blessing Life?

May I see your crystal goblets," asked the well-dressed man as he entered the jewelry store.

"Certainly, sir, they are right over here," replied the clerk.

"I want a particular kind of goblet," the man explained. "I don't use them as drinking glasses; I use them as musical instruments. I need one that sounds the note A 440 vibrations a second."

"You are certainly welcome to check out all the goblets," the clerk commented, "but I haven't any idea in the world which ones are one note and which are another. Take all the time you need."

"It won't take long," the man said.

So saying, the customer took from his pocket a tuning fork. He struck it sharply until it was vibrating. Then he set it on the countertop so that it would set up reverberations. Next, he walked around the store and listened to the glasses. Every goblet that was tuned to the frequency of 440 vibrations a second was resonating. That is the law of harmonics. Things tuned to the same pitch respond to each other.

For this reason people who are tuned to blessing attract other blessing people—and they all attract blessings. In the same way, people who broadcast negative signals find all kinds of negative things coming to them.

Job said it clearly. "The thing that I greatly feared is come upon me" (Job 3:25).

Springfield, Ohio, is known for two products, International Harvester products and Marie Barnhart. It would be worth a trip to Springfield to meet Marie. She was born near the end of the nineteenth century, but she radiates a kind of perpetual youthfulness that makes her seem ageless. Her life is a blessing, a benediction.

If I have made it sound as though she is some kind of gray-plaster saint, I have misled you. For forty or more years she has taught a class of forty or more junior-high girls. She is about as old fashioned as high button shoes, but every generation of teen-agers thinks she is one of them.

While my daughter was in junior high school, Marie came to visit us. The combination worked all over again. Lori thought there was no one like Marie Barnhart. If I asked Marie her secret she simply said, "I really love those girls—they are so precious."

But there is more to Marie. She blesses not only kids, but also tomato plants.

It is interesting that the people who know most about the power of thinking positively and of blessing things are the most eager to learn more about it. So it was not surprising that when I was lecturing in Springfield, Marie Barnhart was right there in one of the front seats. One day she invited me to lunch. This is one of the fringe benefits of the blessing life: blessing people are attracted to you. Sometimes these people are good cooks as well.

As we drove Marie confessed to me, "I have known Psalm 103 most of my life, but I never thought about it the way you have described it. It is wonderful. I think I am understanding something about myself. I always wondered why people turn and smile at me, even when I walk down the street of a strange city."

As we sat at the kitchen table she asked me if I liked home-grown tomatoes. I indicated that I did. She brought a tomato out of the refrigerator. It was almost as big as a cantaloupe.

"This one weighs four pounds," she said proudly.

That was more tomato than I planned to eat. So she rummaged around and found a two-pound tomato that looked small by comparison.

"Could you tell me about your tomatoes?" I asked.

"It may seem foolish to some people, but while I am working in my garden I sing and pray," she said. "I suppose I talk to my plants and sort of encourage them. Anyway, they seem to grow better.

"Beside this," she continued, "I always buy my tomato plants from a Wesleyan Methodist man who goes up and down the rows of plants in his greenhouse and sings. The tomato plants I get from him always seem to do better."

Our meal continued with more conversation like this. Sometimes I wonder if I am a teacher or the student. I hope I am both.

Blessing and Positive Thinking

Jack is an insurance man in Oklahoma City. He told me his method of "self-starting." Each morning he rises, showers, has breakfast, and then puts a phonograph record on the stereo system. To the stirring tones of "Under the Double Eagle" or "Stars and Stripes Forever," he marches out to meet the world of potential insurance customers.

"There is only one problem," he confided. "I know that this is a game I play with myself. I have to put the record on and I have to keep on doing it."

Jack's problem is one we all have. This is the reason for

the magic of blessing. This is not an exercise in self-starting or self-help. It is not another program of auto-suggestion. These systems are good and obviously helpful to millions of people. Perhaps they are beginning courses that prepare us for the life of blessing, but they are certainly not the same thing.

The life of blessing must begin with God. In a short time we will discuss the specific way to bless God as the Bible asks us to do in thirty-three specific places. The important thing is to get your mind and attitude flowing in the direction that God's mind flows.

Once that important step is taken, you are ready to bless yourself. Obviously the attitude of God toward you is a positive one. If any one message shines through the Bible it is that God loves you. Facing the fact that he does, it seems logical to think that you ought to feel the same way about yourself. While it seems obvious that people are concerned about themselves, it does not follow that they feel good about themselves—that they like being who they are.

Strange as it seems, there is no way to ignore yourself. If you are told to forget yourself, the simple command centers your attention on you more than ever. Suddenly you are forced to think why it is so difficult to forget yourself. You have the same problem as the mule that is tied to a tree; he wants to get free, and so he walks around the tree trying to find a way of escape. All of the time he is winding himself closer to the tree—his prison.

Anyone trying to escape from his or her own self-hood becomes terribly self-conscious doing it. The only answer to this problem is to learn to bless yourself. This will make possible the third level of achievement—the art of blessing others. That is the goal of the blessing life. It is an end, not a beginning.

While the idea may seem strange to you if you have tried to become less selfish, it fits rather well into the comment of Jesus when he was asked, "What is the first and great commandment?" He said, "Thou shalt love the Lord thy

God with all thy heart and with all thy soul, and with all thy mind; and thy neighbor as thyself" (Luke 10:27). That makes sense.

If you are full of self-hatred, if you literally curse who you are, it is not likely that you will overflow with love or blessing for anyone else.

The path is clear. We will start walking on it. We will talk about blessing God; then we will discuss blessing ourselves and finally we will talk about blessing other people.

I must issue a stern warning. Do not try to change this orderly process. Do not skip to the self-help section and imagine that you will avoid thinking about God. You must work with the formula. Good cooks know the importance of following directions. If you are making a cake and include everything but baking powder, both your reputation and the cake will fall flat.

There are good reasons for doing things the way I suggest. Thousands of people all over the world can testify that this system works. It may take a while to retrain your thoughts, but persist and it will work.

I heard of a man who wrote to Sears and Roebuck as follows: "Dear Sir, Please send me the one-cylinder gasoline engine described on page 847 of your fall catalog. If it is any good I will send you a check." A reply came: "Dear Sir. The engine is good. Please send check. If it is any good, we will send the engine." In the words of another, "The gospel has not been tried and found wanting; it has been found difficult and not tried."

There is a difference, however, in your beginning the life of blessing. Though you may enter it with some doubting, it is so simple to try and so exciting to use that you will want to make it a permanent life-style whether or not it produces any miracles in your life. It is almost as though you were to learn that eating German chocolate cake and ice cream was the perfect reducing diet.

Start—please do. But remember the Marcie principle: "You gotta be four before you can be five."

Let's Think about God

I Seem to Be a Verb is the title of a book by Buckminster Fuller. This title appeals to me because it helps me to understand myself. It also helps me to know more about God.

Putting God into a static word like a noun is like trying to crowd a sunrise into an eight-by-ten frame. He doesn't fit. God doesn't fit into any of our attempts to explain him. Thinking about God is not easy, but we must think about God.

Although no person has seen God at any time (John 1:18), almost everyone has some idea of what God looks like. For some he is a bewhiskered grandfather, smiling and indulgent. For others he is a brilliant shining light. For still others he is a kind of power, like electricity, but not exactly, of course.

I heard of one man who thought of God as a great big staring eye. That is a horrible picture, but let me tell you how he got it.

As a young boy he lived on a farm. Along with his father he worked in the fields. The father, a stern taskmaster, never allowed his sons to shirk. Even when he had to go into the barn to get something, he had a method of control. Conveniently enough, he had a glass eye. Taking this glass eye out of its socket and laying it on top the fence post, he would warn, "I am going into the barn but I will still be watching you."

Years later in adolescence, the young son came across a verse in the Bible: "The eyes of the Lord are in every place, beholding the evil and the good" (Prov. 15:3). Reading that verse was like turning a key in the storehouse of memory. All the feelings of resentment that were stored since childhood came flooding out. "Is God really like my father's watchful eye?" he asked. "How could a God like that love me. Or, perhaps more to the point, how could I love him?"

How difficult it would be for that man to bless God! If God were a celestial radar scanning the earth for signs of human weakness, who could love him?

Each of us is faced with a problem. We know we cannot make any accurate image of God—even though our mind thinks in pictures—yet we must think of God in some way. If we cannot think of him, how can we bless him?

The ancient Hebrew poem gives us a plan. So we shall look at Psalm 103 in the Old Testament. As you read this outline, it will be helpful to have your own copy of the Scriptures in front of you. In no way is this book an attempt to take the place of the actual reading of the Scripture itself. Quite the contrary. This outline of a journey that I have taken and encouraged thousands of others to take is merely a diary. The Bible itself is the map.

Truthfully God is a verb. He described himself to Moses by saying, "I Am." He acts. He is known by the way he acts. While we can never understand the complete nature of God—although all the religions of the world try—we can learn a great deal about him by seeing what he does. He does what he does because of who *he* is. We learn about the *who* by examining the *what*.

There is one more problem. Even though we are trying to think about the ways God feels and acts, we are limited to our own experiences and our own vocabulary. It is as though we are trying to describe Niagara Falls when all we have seen is a leaking faucet.

Maybe it is like trying to view a mountain through a keyhole. Our view is limited. But it is a start, and you have to start somewhere.

Chapter 6

First Lessons in
God Watching

"I push the blades of grass apart and lay my fingers on God's heart," said Walt Whitman. You might try this. Of course, all that you might see would be the brown earth. After all, you are not Walt Whitman.

Perhaps another figure of speech from the same author will make it easier to begin "God watching."

> I look at the grass,
> Perhaps it is the handkerchief of the Lord,
> Dropped unknowingly by the owner
> With his initial in the corner.

That begins to make sense. The miracle of grass is a way to understand how God acts. It is a miracle of life.

You may not be a nature lover. Grass may not be in your poetic vocabulary. After all, isn't it that irascible herb that turns Saturday mornings into hassles with lawnmowers instead of putters and number three irons? Isn't grass that willful truant that deserts the fertilized lawn to grow luxuriantly in the cracks in the driveway? In that case, Whitman is wasted on you.

There is a picture of God that appeals to everyone. Actually it is not one single view of the Almighty—it is more like a portrait gallery. If you will hang these twelve portraits in your mind, you will fall in love with your heavenly father. These show what he really is.

It shouldn't be difficult to think of your mind as a picture gallery. What else can it be? Learn to walk into this gallery of blessing and spend a few moments each day in front of each of these pictures. You will discover new words to describe the feelings you have. You will search for new meanings in the portraits of God. You may even exclaim in the words of the ecstatic psalmist, "Bless the Lord, O my soul: and all that is within me, bless his holy name." It could be.

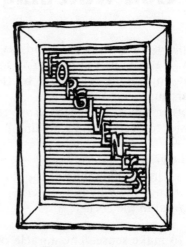

Portrait Number One: Forgiveness

"Who forgiveth all thine iniquities."

—Psalm 103:3

A bright-eyed seven-year-old was asked by her Sunday school teacher, "What is the first thing we must do if we want Jesus to forgive our sins?"

The reply was instant: "You gotta sin."

If we were to understand "iniquities," we might appreciate forgiveness. This somber, old-fashioned word does not fit easily into our modern conversations. If you have a good memory you may recall phrases like "dens of iniquity." This sounds like an opium dispensary in a hide-out for thieves. It might help if we used a modern word, *perversion*.

The Hebrew word from which our English word *iniquity* comes is *Awon,* which means to twist or turn—to take something good and to make evil out of it. It is the wrong turn of the automobile that may disfigure or kill our loved ones.

Sin is like that. Lust is but love turned in the wrong directions. What is greed but ambition that has run astray? What is anger but concern twisted out of shape?

No one has to be convinced that the world in general and each of us in particular has taken a great many wrong turns. A sense of lostness is inevitable. Next comes guilt.

To this heaviness of heart comes the word *forgiveness*. Someone has commented that poor people have the advantage over rich people because they know the joy of struggling with a debt for a long time and then getting it paid. That is a good feeling.

Everyone has sinned. So forgiveness is sweet for everyone. God forgives.

Can you remember when you experienced forgiveness at any level? Someone has said, "Forget it. It's all right." Maybe you felt the emotions of forgiveness when you were the forgiver, not the one forgiven. To be able to forgive is a greater pleasure than to be forgiven. An ancient proverb says, "He who does not forgive breaks the bridge over which he himself must cross."

If you stand for a few moments in front of the picture of God's forgiveness you will feel a warm glow. It is like standing in front of a roaring fire after you have tramped wearily through a blizzard. It is like finding a cool drink of water when you have been dying of thirst. It is like the bliss of relief when stabbing pain goes away.

Luxuriate in this feeling. Bless God for it. Think of God's

forgiving love as a rushing river. You stand on the river bank and cast your sins one by one into that turbulent rushing stream. While you watch they are carried away, out of sight. They are hurled along pell mell into the sea of his forgetfulness.

"Bless the Lord, who forgiveth all thine iniquities."

Portrait Number Two: Healing

"Who healeth all thy diseases."

—Psalm 103:3

You were designed for health. Every part of your body has tremendous power to restore itself, to heal itself.

We all know this. The difficult queston is, If we are supposed to be well, why are so many people sick? Why do hospitals spread like overnight mushrooms all across the country?

These are good questions. They deserve a good answer.

What is now called psychosomatic medicine (the influence of the mind on the body) is recognized by every school child. It is a shocking fact that this truth was ignored until the early part of the twentieth century. We are talking about more than this when we talk about God's power to heal—we are talking about heavenly intervention in our earthly system.

Even so, it is remarkable that David, the shepherd-king who lived a thousand years before the time of Christ, recognized the relationship between the attitudes of mind and the condition of the body. He listed healing immediately following forgiveness.

Through the inspiration that underlies all Scripture, this important idea has been preserved for us. Iniquity is the forerunner of disease. Modern science is doing extensive research to discover the exact relationship between stress (twisting, pressure, tension) and sickness. Everything that is written seems like a simple commentary on ancient Bible truths.

This does not mean that sick people have consciously and deliberately sinned and are bearing the weight of God's anger. Oh no. The exact opposite is true.

The misguided steps of people have taken them away from God's planned abundance; they have missed health. (In a sense that is a kind of sin because the principle word in the Bible for sin is *Hamartia,* which means "to miss the mark.") Sickness and sin are related. The good news is—and what wonderful news it is—that God is so eager to heal their diseases that he deals with the errors that caused them. He forgives their iniquity.

God loves sick people as they are. But he loves them too much to leave them that way.

Above the door of the Harvard Medical School is the motto "Physicians dress the wound; God heals it." Most medical doctors know this. There is a force for healing that is constantly working within us. Often there is an assist from a dedicated medical team, but all the healing has to come from nature. And nature is just the habitual behavior of God, the way he acts.

How do you visualize healing? How do you paint a picture of this miracle power?

Remember falling down on the sidewalk when you were a child? You skinned your knee. In a few days a scab formed and healing was under way. Or perhaps you have had surgery. Stitches closed the wound and healing took place. Much of the healing was visible; much of it was not. Remember how quietly and comfortingly the doctors and nurses moved among the patients of the hospital. For some there was medicine to relieve raging fever; for others there were words of encouragement and information. God is like that. He is a great physician.

Maybe you will want to think of the healing of the earth after it has been ravaged by war. Carl Sandburg's poem *Grass* may help you.

> Pile the bodies high at Austerlitz and Waterloo
> Shove them under and let me work—
> I am the grass; I cover all.

Nature heals the ravaged earth.

Healing is a beautiful word. Behind healing is God. Think about it. Bless God for it. The more you affirm the healing of God, the more you will experience it.

As this experiment in the life of blessing continues, I will tell many stories of ways this healing principle works. For the moment, let me encourage you not to try to understand it. Simply be glad that there is a healing power in the world. Bless God for it.

Portrait Number Three: Redemption

"Who redeemeth thy life from destruction."

—Psalm 103:4

What happens if wrong thinking, wrong living (iniquity), and disease have destroyed us? Is it ever too late to get better? The Bible uses the word *redeem* to describe the process by which a miraculous, almost unbelievable change can take place.

Part of the problem for most of us is that we don't know what to expect because we don't know what we have lost. In a world of unredeemed people, we compare ourselves with our contemporaries. The result? We think we are normal when we are merely average. There is a difference.

My friend Ewald Wolfram is a veritable oracle of down-to-earth proverbs. His unconventional approach to life has startled thousands of people into the strange exercise of

50

thinking. Out of the "Oracles of Ewald" comes the following: "The average person in America has 1.9 legs."

Once you have furrowed your brow and tried to understand whether or not you read correctly, he explains, "Obviously most of us are born with two legs. Some are not. Other people lose legs in accidents or in surgery. Those sad facts are going to change the average. To get the average, we simply divide the number of legs there are by the number of people having them. The answer? Strange but true, the average person in America has 1.9 legs."

This is the average, understand. That is not normal. That certainly is not what God intended. It is important for us to understand what we are supposed to be if we want to know what we can be.

For the person skilled in blessing there needs to be another sentence: "When we recognize what we don't have we know what we *will* have. That is the purpose of redemption.

Redemption means that whatever has been lost by either disobedience or ignorance can be restored. Locked within each of us is the eternal memory of a heavenly plan.

Stop now and underscore that sentence; it can change your life.

If, then, we are going to see a restoration of that original purpose of the Almighty, what will it be? What kind of picture will we paint to help us visualize God in his work of redeeming people? It may be that when you try to think of the back-to-normal picture of yourself you draw a blank. But that is not necessarily bad.

Think of your mind as a piece of canvas stretched on a frame. It is ready for a painting. Now let your imagination go as wild as it will. Try to reconstruct the thoughts of God as he pondered the creation of humanity. What did he want?

Let your faith paint the picture, not your mirror. Don't think of what you have become; think of what you were planned to be.

While scientists are not the final authorities, they sometimes show a greater respect for the creativeness of God than people who talk glibly about the conflict between science and religion.

People who study the human mind marvel at it. Recently such a group affirmed, "The average human mind is capable of learning to read, write, and speak twenty-five different languages. The average human mind could memorize the entire Bible or the complete *Encyclopedia Britannica.*"

How much have we lost when we can't remember our mother-in-law's phone number or the pledge to the flag?

How quickly we settle for mediocrity when God intended excellence. "I will praise thee; for I am fearfully and wonderfully made; marvelous are thy works" (Ps. 139:14).

How can you visualize redemption? While I certainly do not want to minimize the work of Jesus in his crucifixion and resurrection, I realize that for many people this does not explain redemption. There must be a theology first. It is important. Perhaps you will come to that profound theological affirmation in time to come. We cannot assume that everyone who reads these words is at that point now.

A simple start at picturing redemption would be to imagine a destitute artist who had labored for years on a painting. Many times he has refused offers to buy it. He cannot sell it; it is too much a part of him. Finally in his hunger he takes it to a pawn shop where he is given a few dollars for it. He does not forget it. He plans to return and get it some day.

Finally the poor artist is given a job for which he is paid lavishly. He hurries to the pawn shop. In return for the few dollars he is given his picture again. Redemption is like that.

Whatever may be your mental or physical condition at this moment, be assured that God is trying to give you back all your have lost. Bless this part of his nature.

Portrait Number Four: Victory

"[He] crowneth thee with lovingkindness and tender mercies."

—Psalm 103:4

What a good feeling it is to win. What a depressing feeling it is to be a loser.

Many struggles seem common to all people. Even the most devoted and optimistic believer is not exempt. I do not pretend that you will be. But that is not bad news.

It may be that you are going to have struggles with money, family, or health. The important thing is that God has promised you victory. Each moment is bringing you closer to the winner's circle. That faith will sustain you.

Stories from concentration camps and prisons have shown us that no matter how unrealistic hope seemed to be, as long as prisoners retained that hope they could survive torture and deprivation. With no more clothes, food, or comforts than other hopeless prisoners, the hopeful ones survived. Faith in an ultimate victory is a powerful force.

This is not a theory. It is not a dream. While there are as many interpretations of the Bible as there are persons reading it, there is one thing on which everyone must agree: those who trust in God are promised victory. God is a God of victory.

Now, here is what you must do. You must compose your own picture of victory. Have you had a moment of triumph in your life? Remember it. Was it a race you won while you were in high school? Was it the time you moved to the head of the class in a spelling contest? Was it the time you carried the football over the line for the winning touchdown? And what about the time you realized that you had finally conquered a bad habit? Whatever it was, remember the glow.

May I tell you about my personal picture of victory? At one time in my life I felt I had more wars than I had weapons. I felt myself slowly turning into a loser. To lose once in a while is not bad; to become a loser is fatal.

Help came. It came in the form of a tiny snapshot taken in Paris. Frank Lowe was showing me the tourist attractions of this world-famous city. When we came to the Arc de Triomphe, the magnificent gateway built to celebrate Napoleon's successful return from battle, he insisted that I have my picture made. So the picture was made and I forgot it.

One day the picture turned up. It was yellowing with age, but it brought to mind again the youthful exuberance and enthusiasm I had in those days. I remembered, too, the words of St. Paul as he talked about the normal attitude of a believer: "Now thanks be unto God, which always causeth us to triumph in Christ" (2 Cor. 2:14). That was the feeling I wanted to have.

I remember feeling a little foolish as I took the yellowing photograph and pasted it on the front of a file drawer in my office. As I sat at my desk I could look at it. Victory. Victory. I am standing under the arch of triumph; I cannot fail. The feeling of victory is a delicious feeling. It can be yours.

You will have to construct your own picture of victory. Whether it is landing the biggest contract of your career, snagging a giant trout, hitting the ball over the fence, or reaching a spiritual victory—paint the picture in vivid colors on your mind. Put that picture in your blessing gallery. Now spend a while thanking God for the feeling you had.

It feels good, doesn't it? Don't forget how it feels. Bless God for the promise of victory in other things. Remember, "He crowneth thee."

Portrait Number Five: Satisfaction

"Who satisfieth thy mouth with good things; so that thy youth is renewed like the eagle's."

—Psalm 103:5

Recently my wife asked me to read a story in one of her household magazines. It might be called heavy reading because it told the story of a woman who lost more than four hundred pounds of excess weight. If it hadn't been so tragic, it would have been humorous. Anyone who has struggled to lose a few extra pounds can certainly sympathize with anyone who had to lose a fifth of a ton of weight. Life was miserable for this woman. To take a bath in a tub meant that she could put only two inches of water in the tub or it would overflow when she got in.

When finally this heroic woman was able to trace the roots of her uncontrollable hunger she found that her childhood was filled with dissatisfaction and hunger.

Apparently she and her brother lived a very painful life because of the alchoholism of their mother. She made them wait for her in the car while she spent her time in the tavern getting drunk. Once in a while she would bring them a few mouthfuls of food. Sometimes it would be a small bottle of olives—this would be the food for the day.

The children ate anything they could. Even leaves from the trees became part of their food. *If the time ever comes when we can eat all we want, we will never be hungry again.* This thought became an obsession with these troubled children.

When the girl became old enough she found a husband and began to eat. Eating became a passion. Of course, she got fat.

How did she lose all this weight? Her satisfactions had to change. It was that simple.

While we are not talking about being overweight, it is interesting to notice that doctors often say that people eat not to satisfy their nutritional needs, but their emotional hungers. In any event, *satisfaction* is a wonderful word. It means that there is just the right amount. There is not too much. There is not too little.

As you observe the religious practices of people, does it occur to you that many religious ideas seem to operate on a mood of quiet desperation? As you reach one level of achievement someone raises the standard. As you cross the goal line someone moves the goal posts. You never quite catch up. It is as though you had to feel mildly guilty all the time in order to be holy.

Whatever happened to the rest for your soul that Jesus promised? The rest is still available. God is the God of adequacy. If you are frustrated and dissatisfied, begin now to bless the source of adequacy that God will give you.

If you feel like the mother who complained, "I feel like a six-piece pie that is being served to ten people," there is hope. Walk into your blessing gallery and think of your picture of satisfaction. Put a frame around that picture and gaze at it. In case you cannot think of any pictures, here are some suggestions:

1. Picture the ocean as it washes against the shoreline. How big is it? How deep? How much energy does it have? How long has it been there? How long will it be there? The answer is: enough. It is big enough, deep enough, old enough, and energetic enough. I can remember the little boy who had been raised in poverty. Seeing the ocean for the first time he exclaimed, "This is the first time I have seen anything there is enough of." There is abundance.

2. When I think of "enough" I remember being at the well in Samaria. As every Bible student knows, Jacob's well is there. It was here that Jesus said to a Samaritan woman who had come to draw water, "Whoever drinks of this water shall thirst again, but whoever drinks of the water that I shall give him shall never thirst."

The scene is easy to remember as you watch tourists come and go. Most of them want to taste that water. If I am leading a group, I always see that each person has a cup— even if I have to show them how to make a cup out of a piece of notebook paper. It is important to me that they taste this water that still flows freely just as it has for thousands of years.

On a recent visit to Israel we saw a large group of tourists from Poland. They seemed particularly reverent. This particular place in their pilgrimage was extremely important to them. Not only did they avidly drink from the well, using the small cups they had brought from home, but most of them brought plastic jugs and bottles so that they could carry gallons of this sparkling water back to Poland.

I was surprised and impressed. Then I reasoned that this kind of activity must go on year after year. Yet the well does not run dry. No one will exhaust it. This has become one of my pictures in my gallery of blessings.

Of course the best kind of picture for you to hang in your gallery of blessing is one that brings a strong emotional feeling to you. Looking at this picture should give you the feeling of being satisfied, of having enough.

That is the nature of God. Bless him for being like that.

Portrait Number Six: Renewal

"So that thy youth is renewed like the eagle's."

—Psalm 103:5

Youth. That is the magic word. Someone observed humorously that American women at thirty look as though they were forty because they begin to worry at twenty how they are going to look at fifty.

I do not believe this is true, but it does at least hint at the mania for renewal. Highly paid writers who compose advertising material that must sell merchandise say that there are eleven magic words in selling. One is *new*. People love what is new.

The innocent adjective *old* is usually seen in poor company. Who has not read of a "crabby *old* man"? Surely there are some disagreeable *young* men, aren't there? In the stories it is always the *old* miser. Why? Is he a miser because he is old or is he old because he is a miser?

Even God does not like to be labeled "old." When revealing his name to Moses he said, "I Am" (Exod. 3:14). So insistent was the Almighty that he repeated this fact. Whatever else God may be, he is, as Walter Horton described him, "our eternal contemporary."

An interesting problem faces us as we think about the renewing power of God. If, as scientists claim, our bodies replace their elements at least every seven years, and some of the elements of our bodies are replaced every twenty-four hours or less, why do we age? Why do we continue building the new parts of our bodies like the defective old ones?

For example, if a man has heart trouble at the age of forty and in seven years all the elements of his heart have replaced themselves, why does he still have a leaky valve on his forty-seventh birthday?

Perhaps I can put the problem another way. If I were to offer a thousand dollars to anyone who could grow an old leaf on a tree, who would claim the reward? *You can never grow old. You can only grow new.*

You cannot grow an old hair on your head. You cannot grow an old fingernail. We always grow new.

57

Does this aspect of God's provision for you make you happy? It should. The Greek word translated "gospel" in your Bible is literally the good *news,* not the good old.

How can you make yourself conscious of this tremendous power? What kind of picture will you paint for your gallery of blessing—a picture that will make you *feel* the surging newness of the life that is stretching out in front of you?

Can you remember the ruddy newness of a newly born infant? Every child that is born is a reminder that God has not despaired of the human race.

Think about the crocuses or tulips pushing through the snow with the flaming yellow and red blossoms. Think of June in New England:

> What is so rare as a day in June,
> Then, if ever, come perfect days.
> The heaven tries earth if it be in tune,
> And over it warmly her soft ear lays.
> Whether we look or whether we listen
> We hear life murmur or see it glisten.
> Every clod feels a stir of might,
> An instinct within it reaches and towers,
> And reaching blindly above it for light
> Climbs to a soul in grass and flowers.

Has something happened to you that has plunged you into a whole new world? You felt the past was thrown off like the golden locks that lay on the barber's floor after your first haircut. Can you capture again the feeling of freedom with your first pair of sneakers after a long summer of going barefoot?

Whatever it is that can paint a scene of newness on your mind, capture that feeling. Frame it. Put it in your gallery of blessings. "Behold I make all things new," says God.

There is no way you can hang an actual portrait of God in your gallery, but when you think of newness, he is not far away. Bless him. It is a good feeling.

Chapter 7

More Lessons in God Watching

Portrait Number One: The Ultimate Executive

"The Lord executeth righteousness and judgment for all that are oppressed."

—Psalm 103:6

The phrase "ultimate executive" has developed a new meaning for me. In recent years I reluctantly left the pastorate I had served for twenty-one years. I assumed the position of executive in a Christian organization. It called for new skills. It was a brand-new world. I had to learn, in fact, what an executive is.

Essentially I was told, "An executive is one who gets things done." He doesn't necessarily do them himself but he must see that the right things get done at the right time. That involves working *with* people, not merely working for them.

Soon my bookshelf groaned under a load of new books describing the effective executive. Not only were the dust jackets of these books different; the ideas within them were different as well. I kept looking for the things that *all* of them said, the common denominator of executive success.

Finally I found the unifying principle: Build on your strengths, not your weaknesses. Discover the strengths of others and build on them.

Does God do that? Exactly. Through all the inconsistencies and weaknesses of human beings, God works out his purpose. "All things work together for good to them that love God, to them who are the called according to his purpose" (Rom. 8:28). The world is in good hands.

How do you capture that feeling of confidence that makes it possible for you to bless the Lord "who executes righteousness and judgment for all who are oppressed"? What kind of picture can you frame for your personal gallery of blessing?

If you are a managerial person yourself, you might want to frame a picture like those in the business magazines. An expensively dressed executive is sitting at a large uncluttered desk. He is looking at an array of charts and graphs that show an upward graph-line. Things are going well.

Or you may want a picture of a giant orchestra playing all the instruments yet remaining under the control of the maestro's baton. Harmony is coming out of difference.

Whatever kind of picture you use to set your emotional mood, try to capture the feeling you would have if you were that person. Now bless God because he is in control. Through people—even you—he is getting things done. He is the ultimate executive.

Portrait Number Two: The Revealer

"He made known his ways unto Moses, his acts unto the children of Israel."

—Psalm 103:7

Everybody is a lot like Daniel Defoe's character Robinson Crusoe. We arrive on the earth with little knowledge of the world itself or who manages it, just as Robinson Crusoe landed on a stange island. Of course, Crusoe discovered right away that the island must have been inhabited, because he saw footprints in the sand. Following these he found another human being whom he called Friday, named for the day Crusoe met him.

Our discovery of God is like that. We see evidence of him in the world that he has made, we can literally trace his footprints in the sand. We follow his acts and we find him. According to the Hebrew poet, David, Moses learned of God's nature while the Hebrew people themselves merely know of his acts. It must be clear that God discloses himself to us to the degree that we are ready for that disclosure.

I really don't know what kind of picture to suggest for your blessing gallery. It ought to be a picture that suggests some way that God reveals himself. Perhaps it will be different for all of us. It could be a beautiful scene in the world of nature. Elizabeth Barrett Browning suggests,

> Earth's crammed with heaven,
> And every common bush afire with God;
> But only he who sees, takes off his shoes,
> The rest sit round it and pluck blackberries.

You may want to catch the mood of the time you were desperate to find the answer to some question. Then miraculously God showed you the way to understand. Try to recapture the feeling you had. Remember how all the pieces fell together. It is a wonderful feeling. Thank God for it. Bless him.

Portrait Number Three: Mercy

"The Lord is merciful and gracious, slow to anger, and plenteous in mercy. He will not always chide: neither will he keep his anger forever."

—Psalm 103:8-9

If you want to understand God, you must think of the most merciful thing you know. God is full of mercy. In contrast to the flinty attitude of "getting what is coming to me," Shakespeare observes in *The Merchant of Venice,* "The quality of mercy is not strained. It falls as the gentle dew from heaven."

That is beautiful, but it presents a problem. Who has seen the dew fall? How do you visualize it?

Naturally we can look at the grass that sparkles in the morning sunlight, but that does not really give us a feeling of mercy. Maybe the only way to feel the warmth of mercy is to feel deeply the need of it.

Imagine, for example, that you are a prisoner condemned to die in the gas chamber. For months you have lived with this chilling prospect. Then at the moment of your blackest despair in your gray-barred world you are told of a pardon, your pardon. In that instance you understand the feeling of mercy.

It wasn't as though you did not deserve punishment. Imagine you did. But in spite of your unworthiness you were given a second chance. Does this picture help you to understand God?

"He hath not dealt with us after our sins; nor rewarded us according to our iniquities. For as the heaven is high above the earth, so great is his mercy toward them that fear him."

—Psalm 103:10-11

In order to bless the Lord it is not important that you know *why* God is merciful; it is important that you let yourself luxuriate in the warmth of that mercy.

There are other pictures you can hang in your gallery of blessing. Have you seen a painting of the women inspired by Florence Nightingale? These were women who moved like angels among the suffering men who had been wounded in battle. These women left the perfumed drawing rooms and sought out the hospital wards that were heavy with the odor of death. They were called "angels of mercy." It is a good thing to stand a long time in contemplation of God's mercy. There is nothing we need more. There is no word that can more quickly trigger our gratitude and blessing.

Bless God for his mercy.

Portrait Number Four: Forgetfulness

"As far as the east is from the west, so far hath he removed our transgressions from us."

—Psalm 103:12

> I sit beside my silent fire
> And pray for wisdom yet,
> For wisdom to remember
> And courage to forget.
> —Sara Teasdale

My friends laugh at my lostness most of the time. "How do you expect to show people the way to heaven when you can't find your way to the post office?" they ask.

They have a point. But I have managed to get around in this world in spite of my poor sense of direction.

In 1948 I began a trip around the world. Leaving San Francisco on a slow steamer, Ralph Starr and I made our way to China. Ralph is a born navigator. He can remember every turn in every road. We traveled by ship, plane, truck caravan, and finally by mule back into Tengchung, Yunan, West China. If I were to call him this moment, I feel sure he could describe every pagoda we passed. Not I.

We separated in Tengchung. He remained to help with the work of the hospital and eventually to help missionaries Dr. and Mrs. David Gaulke and Milton and Eleanor Buettner to escape. He was afraid I could not make it on my own. As we separated he gave me simple instructions, "Just keep on going west and you will get home all right."

Twelve months later I did. When I sailed into New York harbor to see if the stone lady was still carrying a torch for me—and for all the other poor, tired, huddled masses—I was still traveling west. When I finally took the Pennsylvania train from New York to Indiana I was still heading west. The east and west never meet.

A few months ago my wife and I were in Alaska. We were told that if we had time we could travel to the Arctic. I am not sure that I really want to do that. I am sure my wife, Berny, would. She has the soul of a gypsy. We did not go.

For a moment let us imagine that we travel north to the North Pole. At the time we cross that point we begin to travel south. Since the world is round, I don't really understand the difference, but it is there anyway. When you go far enough north you start heading south again. You can go east as long as you live and you will never be heading west.

Didn't David say that God has forgiven all our iniquities in the very first part of Psalm 103? Of course. Then why does he come back to talk about our "transgressions." Isn't this just another word for *sin*?

In a general way, yes. More specifically it isn't. *Iniquity* means the unconscious bent to miss the target, to pervert a good thing. *Transgression* is a more vigorous, willful word. It means to "walk across, to violate, to go where you are not supposed to go and do what you are not supposed to do."

This needs a special kind of forgiveness. From a purely human point of view, it is one thing to overlook errors in situations in which people can't help themselves, but it is quite another matter to forgive people who really know better.

Stand for a moment in the warmth of God's mercy. He forgives our transgressions—the things we know we are doing wrong when we do them. The powerful word *atonement* echoes across the centuries. Like the base notes in the "song of redemption," atonement reverberates: "All we like sheep have gone astray; we have turned every one to his own way; and the Lord hath laid on him the iniquity of us all" (Isa. 53:6). What a blessed thought!

Even more thrilling than this is the fact that God forgets. To that never-never point where east and west meet—that is how far he has removed our transgressions from us.

If "to forgive is divine," what word shall we use for *forget*? There is none. Our problem is solved, however, when we realize that *forget* is the flip side of *forgive*. You cannot have one without the other. If forgiveness is real, forgetting is automatic. That is the nature of God. There are no tombstones in the cemetery where God buries our sins. No one can go and dig them up again—not even God himself. Bless him.

It should not be difficult to find pictures to hang in your gallery of blessing—pictures of the wonder of forgiving and forgetting. Perhaps the simple remembrance of the human tendency to forgive but not forget will help us be grateful to God for his kind of forgiveness.

From the human point of view it is easy to bury the hatchet as long as we leave the handle sticking up out of the ground so we can find it again. How different is God's love.

Can you visualize a chalkboard? On it are written all your transgressions. Then a merciful angel comes with an eraser and wipes away every mark. None is visible. But the angel is not satisfied. With a wet sponge she washes the chalkboard one more time, just to be sure. The marks will never be remembered again. Blessed thought.

If you want to be in the mood of blessing God, simply spend a little time in the gallery of blessing looking at some pictures that have come from your own album of "forgiving and forgetting." You will not see the face of God, but you will see his footprints. Walk in them.

Portrait Number Five: A God with Dirty Hands

"He knoweth our frame; he remembereth that we are dust."

—Psalm 103:14

Each of us is a strange mixture of dust and divinity. No matter how hard we may try to deny either part of us, we cannot. If we try to live as though we were totally physical, totally animal, our divinity cries out.

On the other hand, if we try to emphasize our divinity to the extent that we will not admit we are human, our humanity comes bursting through. You might say we are angels with dirty wings.

It is a good thing to remember that while we have trouble keeping these two sides of our nature balanced, God does not. He understands. Bless him. No matter how high we soar in our spiritual ambitions, God always smiles knowingly. Like Daedalus with the wax wings (Remember the man in the Roman legend? He wanted to fly to the sun.), when we get too high our wings droop and we fall to the earth. We are reminded one more time of our humanity. God never forgets. He remembers that we are dust.

I know a "dusty old story" that illustrates this. It is not a dirty story—just dusty.

Five-year-old Jason had been to Sunday school. He was filled with questions. "Mother," he said, "our teacher told us that God made people out of dust. Is this true."

"Yes," she replied. "The Bible says that God made man out of the dust of the earth."

"Our teacher told us that when we die our bodies go back to the dust? Is this true?" the boy asked.

"Yes, that is true, too," the mother replied.

"Well," said the excited Jason, "Come and look under the bed; somebody is either coming or going."

There is a great deal of cleansing in that old story. What a prison we live in when we impose upon ourselves goals that God did not assign us. No wonder people live with the relentless whip of guilt over them. They have forgotten they are human.

If we were to believe all that is written about energy and vitality, we would feel guilty to take a nap.

In a world in which brightly colored books tell us of the "newest path to success and fulfillment," what do we do when our dreams get dusty? What happens when in our spiritual mountain climbing we find dirt under our finger-nails?

In Oklahoma City a very super-energetic, super-striving, super-achieving woman attended my lectures. She absorbed every word I said about blessing. All week long she assured me, "This is my kind of stuff. I love it. This is the way I live. I believe in being positive."

At the close of the last sessions this effervescent young woman confided to me, "I just learned something about myself that I don't like."

"What?" I asked.

"Today I discovered that I am 'down on people' who are 'down on people,' " she replied.

I laughed. That is a great discovery. One of the perils of spiritual achievement is negativism that invades people who are not positive. She was wise to catch that. I admire her.

"That's great," I said. "Now don't get down on yourself because you have discovered that you are down on people who are down on people. You are human."

How do you hang a picture in your gallery of blessing—a picture that will make you feel God's acceptance of your humanity? I really don't know how to visualize this part of God. Maybe you can flash back to the Christmas drama in your local church. Doesn't everyone love the little kid with

her halo on crooked? When the bathrobe-clad youngster standing as the austere Joseph behind the manger waves to the audience and says, "Hi, mom," don't we all enjoy it?

One-hundred-percent divinity is a scratchy garment for us to wear. A little dust on our wings is becoming. We may forget that we are dust. God doesn't. He is not a clinically clean Aunt Matilda. He doesn't rub his hand over our piano to see if it is dusty. He is too busy enjoying the music. Bless him for this.

Portrait Number Six: Sovereignty

"The Lord hath prepared his throne in the heavens; and his kingdom ruleth over all."

—Psalm 103:19

To be godly is a good thing. To be god is deadly. It is a wonderful thing to accept Christ as Messiah, but to have a messiah complex is to have the most complex complex possible. It precludes salvation because we are trying to nail ourselves to a cross so that we can provide our self-won atonement.

To change the figure of speech, an Atlas complex (that is trying to carry the world on our shoulders) is bad both for us and the world. We collapse. So does the world.

We need to think about the sovereignty of God. What an overpowering thought, "The Lord . . . ruleth over all." Sometimes when the headlines are particularly depressing we feel like the poet John Drinkwater: "Right forever on the scaffold/Wrong forever on the throne."

Then, of course, we walk into the gallery of blessing and see as Drinkwater continues: "Yet behind the dim unknown/Standeth God within the shadows/Keeping watch above His own."

The nearsighted believer survives from tremor to tremor. True believers know that they cannot understand all the ways that God works, but they rest in the knowledge that even the shadows that cross their earthly paths are an evidence of light shining somewhere. That's where God is. God is light.

There really doesn't seem to be any way to understand what God is doing. We can simply see what he has done. That fact is tremendously reassuring. As the famous hymn states,

> Hast thou not seen
> How thy desires have been
> Granted in what he ordaineth.

If you do not feel like blessing the Lord for what is in front of you, at least you can bless God for what lies behind you. Soon even the present and the future will be the past. In retrospect you will see that God rules over all. Bless him for it now. Why wait?

Again, the best way to get pictures for your gallery of blessing is to paint them yourself. However, I will suggest a couple of classic ones.

How about the picture of the heavenly weaver? The idea is that God is weaving a tapestry of our lives. He takes all the bright, happy things, the somber things, and the in-between things and weaves them on his heavenly loom. Every now and then we look up and try to see what kind of design is emerging. Usually we can't see much beauty.

If we are wise and realize that we are looking at the tapestry from the bottom side, we get a different feeling. Some day we are going to see things from God's side. There will be revealed a fantastic design, a composite of all the good and bad of our life.

How do you make this image work for you? How do you let it become the tuning fork that adjusts the tune of your life?

Keep remembering that when your life is parallel to the will of God, when your thoughts run in the same direction as God's, he reinforces your feelings. (Technically this is called faith.) New power flows into your emotions. You feel the energizing power of blessing. In a little while you will recognize the blessing itself. Right now you are simply setting the stage for God to work.

As I write these words I am sitting in the airport in Chicago. A flight was delayed. I had been scheduled to arrive in Indianapolis last night, but something went wrong with the plane. That didn't disturb me. I would much rather have it happen while the plane is on the ground than when it is thirty thousand feet in the air.

Because of the delay I had to spend the night and part of the morning in a hotel somewhere in Chicago. I worked. I worked late last night and early this morning. A little while ago I called the office to tell them of my delay. They cannot see me working here at the hotel desk, but I have been working nevertheless. In a few hours they will see some of the results of my work. Now they cannot.

I am not suggesting that there is anything particularly godlike in using my delays for a constructive purpose, but it does help me to understand that God works to accomplish his purposes even when we don't see it happening at the moment.

I am sure that caterpillars do not have psychiatrists to comfort them in their discouraging hours inside the slender dark cocoon that is their prison. They really do not need encouragement. It is their nature not to give up.

In the event there were some way to tell the caterpillar of its ultimate destiny—to become a shining butterfly—such encouragement might make it difficult to wait. An early exit from the cocoon would be fatal. Relax and let it happen, caterpillar. Relax, believer. We are promised that "the Lord hath prepared his throne in the heavens; and his kingdom ruleth over all."

In your personal gallery of blessings you need to frame the most vivid pictures you can—pictures of the sovereignty of God. In the event you can't dream up an effective picture, let me plant a few seeds in your mind:

1. The chambermaid sees only the messy paint pots and the unfinished canvas; the artist sees the finished picture in his or her mind. Trust the artist, not the maid.

2. The ditchdigger sees only the hole in the ground; the architect dreams of the finished home. Trust the architect.

3. The baking powder and the eggs have left their comfortable and secure world of box and shell. They have a feeling that they exist in a mixed-up, confused world. The cook's eyes are bright as she thinks of the smiling faces of the people singing "Happy Birthday" to a surprised father. Trust the cook.

4. Workers in the quarry see only a large chunk of damaged marble. It is in their way. Michaelangelo sees the marble and sees within it an angel that needs only to be released by his chisel. Trust Michaelangelo.

Remember that learning to bless the Lord is not to try to understand him. It is not to imagine what God looks like, whether he is black or white, with or without substance. It is enough that you understand how he works. When your mind is rejoicing in God's overarching design, you are as close as it is safe to get. Be glad.

Don't try to absorb all of these lessons on God-watching at once. Maybe you ought to take these ideas and think about them one day at a time. Let your mind catch the mood, the attitude, the feeling. Think of all the ways you have seen these principles operate in the world.

If you stumble upon a rushing stream of new ideas, put your little sailboat into it and let it go as far as it can. Use your imagination. J. B. Phillips contends that "your God is too small." Maybe you need a new picture. Maybe you ought to let the picture grow to its full size before you frame it.

Chapter 8

A Little Story about Fence Posts and Telephone Lines

North Carolinians have an almost frantic loyalty to their state. One of their most devoted sons, Prince Deal, told me, "God must have a special love for North Carolina. Why else would he make the sky "North Carolina Blue"?

I like North Carolina myself. It seems to have the kind of soil in which my ideas sprout easily. I enjoyed giving my lectures on blessing to the people in Drexel, North Carolina.

One evening I sat with a group in the home of Lewis Sigmon. Lewis's wife, Thera, was patiently explaining to anyone who would listen how excited she was to discover the Parallel Principle.

"We learned that if you get a wire to be parallel to those overhead wires that carry electricity, even though the wire is not connected to anything, it will pick up an electrical current. I never knew that before."

Lewis, the husband and patient listener, spoke. "That is right."

O course, I was glad to hear him confirm my illustration, since he is an electrical contractor and understands those things.

He continued. "I haven't thought about it for a long time, but I remember my years as a soldier. We were in Italy. Since I was in the Signal Corps I had to string the wire for the field telephones so that we could stay in touch with the soldiers at the front. Naturally we didn't have time to put up large poles, so we strung the wire on top of the fence posts.

"All at once the phone started ringing. When we picked it up to listen we discovered that no one was calling. It was eerie.

"Then we looked up. We hadn't noticed it before, but the fence posts we used were directly under power lines. They were parallel. They became electrified even though they were not connected."

That fence post story ought to help you understand the principle: Prayer is not our overcoming the reluctance of God. It is merely our aligning with the willingness of God.

When we use the words *the will of God,* we sometimes make it sound as though God is going to do something for us whether we want it or not. Can you imagine God saying, "I am going to make you well no matter how much you want to be sick"? Hardly.

What can we do? Since it is the nature of God to bless, let your mind flow with this powerful current. If your thoughts are negative they are at cross purposes with him.

In the Book of Job, we find an interesting phrase: "Agree with God and be at peace; therefore good shall come to thee" (22:21). These words are ancient ones. I didn't invent the idea of paralleling the will of God; I'm simply writing about it.

Your mind has tremendous power. Why not make it work for you?

If you have trouble getting your mind to stay in one place long enough to do any good, I have good news for you. In a few moments I am going to give you my guaranteed formula for getting your mind on a leash so that you can lead it where you want it to go.

For now, let's do a little drawing on the tablecloth. Draw some telephone poles and some power lines. Please do not simply look at my illustration. Do your own. It shouldn't be hard to improve on mine.

Now comes the exciting part. While you try to visualize the power of God, which is just another name for the nature of God, change your drawing. Hang the twelve portraits from your personal blessing gallery in the two previous chapters on the overhead wires. It will look a little strange, but do it anyway.

You have moved your gallery of blessing pictures out of your confined mental room and have hung them in space, like pictures suspended on the power lines you have drawn. Good. You have made the first and most important step. Pictures are static; they make things stand still. They freeze the action. But this is unnatural. Life is never standing still. Neither is God.

Such is the reason for the second of the Ten Commandments: "Thou shalt not make unto thee any graven image." How does that relate to making images such as pictures?

Obviously it has a great deal to do with this. Neither God nor life itself is static. But in order to think about them, we have to get them to stand still long enough to look at them.

Actually all these pictures are reminders of the pulsating presence of God with all his attributes.

It is a little like the pictures of your child or your grandchild that you carry in your wallet. The beautiful picture is impressive, but it is no substitute for the real thing, the laughing bundle of love.

God is bigger than any frame we can put him into.

When we admit this, we are ready for the magic, or should I say miracle. Something is going to happen.

As soon as we get our mind thinking in the direction that God works, something tremendous is going to happen. The power of all these "ways God works" descend on us. Their power starts to work on us. Then it starts to work in us. All we have to do is get lined up—to get in parallel. As we have said, to those who believe, no explanation is necessary; to those who do not believe, no explanation is possible.

Personally, I am glad that it works because I have been able to use these ideas in unbelievable ways. I have fantastic stories to tell. Whether or not you can believe these stories is not important. Trust the ideas. Soon you will have your own fantastic stories to tell.

Warning: If you attempt to use this power selfishly, it will destroy you. That sounds ominous, but it is nonetheless truthful.

Just as electricity that comes from a major overhead source to a secondary wire must be grounded or drained off into the earth or it will kill people, so God's blessings must be applied to worthwhile purposes. That becomes phase three of the blessing life: how to bless other people, situations, and things. It is important. It is necessary, but it can wait. It will have to. It is a result, not a resolution.

Let us talk about blessing ourselves.

Chapter 9

Learning How to Bless Ourselves

Dean Inge, noted bishop of England, once observed: "Every man must be his own center, but he is not obliged to be his own circumference."

You are the key. You have to start with yourself, but you can't end there.

"Though the whole round earth be filled with good," observed Ralph Waldo Emerson, "no kernel of nourishing corn can come to a man except from that portion of ground which God has given him to till." There are simpler ways to say this, I am sure. I remember seeing a plaque on a kitchen wall: "Bloom where you are planted."

To suggest this idea always seems sub-Christian. Our standard instruction appears to be, get out and do something for someone and you will feel better. The idea seems to be good, but we seldom examine it. When we do, we realize that Jesus was saying almost the opposite.

"Thou shalt love the Lord thy God with all thy heart and with all thy soul and with all thy mind . . . and thou shalt love thy neighbor as thyself," the Scripture tells us. If the mind is full of self-dislike, rejection, and failure, there is no likelihood that it will overflow with love, acceptance, and encouragement for other people.

One day a young mother burst into my office. Her tearful face told me her story even before she spoke. But her words were even more eloquent: "My husband has just told me that he does not love me. If he ever did he does not now."

"I don't blame him," I said as she shuffled across the floor to a waiting chair.

"Pardon me," she replied. "I don't think I understood you."

"I don't blame your husband for not loving you," I repeated. Then, speaking as softly and encouragingly as I could, I continued, "I know it sounded terrible for me to say that I don't blame your husband for not loving you. Maybe I should have said, 'I can understand how he feels.' You see everything you have said by your actions and the tone of your voice has told me that you do not love yourself. You seem to dislike your face, your figure, your life-style, and the fact that you got married at all."

Slowly the truth of these statements filtered into her mind.

"What can I do?" she asked.

"There is only one thing you can do," I suggested. "You need to start by reminding yourself that God loves you—he really does. He created you with a purpose and a reason. You are like nobody else in all the world. In spite of your failures, your heartaches, and your rejection, God still loves you. This is where you have to start."

I continued, "God loves you just as you are, but too much to let you stay that way. You can begin by saying that since God knows you better than you know yourself, you ought to accept yourself, even love yourself. Bless yourself. You will be surprised how other people's attitudes toward you change."

Self-hatred builds a barrier that keeps out God's love, and the love of other people as well.

Somewhere I heard the statement "It is the normal characteristic of a love-starved person to reject love." The more they need love, the more they seem to turn it away.

Not only is this true, but the locked-up life has to become an open passageway for God to work. Paul affirms this:

"[God] is able to do exceeding abundantly above all that we ask or think, according to the power that worketh in us" (Eph. 3:20). This verse can be the secret of success or the analysis of the cause of failure.

It is certainly true that we are not supposed to be our own circumference, which is the limit of what is happening in our world. It is also true that whatever is going to happen happens first within us.

Not long ago a group of Christian leaders met to talk about ways to communicate their faith. The session was to be very open and nonthreatening. Each person was asked to be accepting and forgiving. No one was to criticize.

Each leader was given a piece of paper and told, "In the next three minutes write down all the things you do not like about yourself." At the end of the three minutes the sheets were turned in and the results tabulated. A few of the persons were still writing frantically when the bell rang.

The results? The average number of "things I do not like about myself" was fifteen.

Then these same poeple were told to list fifteen good things about themselves. The same three-minute limit was used. At the end of the three minutes no one had found fifteen things for which he or she could be thankful or glad about. Some found none. The average was three.

While I was not present at this session, which was reported in *Faith and Work* magazine, I have used the story as an illustration in my lectures. Strangely, when I ask my audience to guess the number of positives and negatives that the experimental group discovered, the estimates are about the same. This says something about the people who made the estimates; they feel nearly the same way about themselves.

Thinking evil of yourself almost seems a requirement for helping others to think well of themselves, and to believe that God loves them. But if we are secretly convinced that God is ashamed of us, how can we convince others that God loves them, or that they can love others?

Today I saw a sign cleverly painted on a rough wooden plaque: "Bless this lousy apartment." I smiled a painful

smile. It is impossible to be positive and negative at the same time. "Out of the same mouth proceedeth blessing and cursing. My brethren, these things ought not so to be" (James 3:10).

You can smile at this sign. You can laugh at yourself for all the negative feelings you have about yourself. Even if they are disguised as humility, they are pretty ridiculous.

At the center of our new blessing life is the fact that since God is blessing us, we should not contradict him. We should not question his judgment. Awkward as it may be, you are going to have to learn to bless yourself. At least you are going to have to quit cursing yourself and saying mean things about the person whom God loves.

Steering Clear of Negative Thoughts

It seems ages ago that I first saw the book *Psycho-Cybernetics*. It was lying on the table in a dentist's home in Portland, Oregon. When he saw me looking at the book, he asked, "Have you read this book?"

"I can't even pronounce the title," I replied.

So he explained how to pronounce the title. Then he explained how the book came to be written.

Dr. Maxwell Malz, a plastic surgeon, was busy trying to restore the faces and feelings of young men who had been injured in World War I. It was easy to see why these men were self-conscious and why they retreated from life. Their scarred faces made them ashamed. They hid. They refused to go out where the world of people could see them.

Patiently Doctor Malz and other surgeons tried to reconstruct their disfigured faces. Even when they were supremely successful, the problem didn't go away. The newly presentable faces didn't solve the problem. The men still hid and were ashamed. Doctor Malz was puzzled.

An insight came when he went to Germany to study with some of the world's greatest plastic surgeons at the University of Heidelberg. There on the university campus Doctor Malz observed other young men with scars on their faces. They wore them proudly, almost as though they were ornaments.

These scarred German young men were leaders on the campus. They were elected to places of leadership; they were admired by the prettiest girls. They certainly did not regard their faces as hideous.

It became obvious to Doctor Malz and his fellow doctors that the real scars are on the inside of the mind. It doesn't really matter what kind of things are happening on the outside as long as we are directed by what is on the inside.

The idea intrigued Doctor Malz, leading him to make a study of motivation. Out of this study came the term *cybernetics*. The first part of the bigger term that he used, *psycho,* had to do with the mind. *Cybernetics* comes from a Greek word that means "the helmsman or steersman of a ship."

There is a goal-seeking mechanism within us, discovered Doctor Malz. This goal-seeking device brings people to a predetermined goal, a goal they themselves may have put there but never recognized. No matter what the external pressures are, this helmsman steers them straight toward the goal. Doctor Malz's book *Psycho-Cybernetics* is an analysis of how this works.

As I read the book I kept asking a question: Surely the mind is a powerful part of our life. Scientists outdo themselves making estimates of the ultimate capacity of the mind, but how do you give instructions to the helmsman? How do you give him a chart and compass?

It seemed for a while that all I was doing was accumulating facts about how powerful this helmsman is; there seems to be very little help in getting him headed in the right direction.

While I was studying these concepts, I heard a doctor-friend of mine say, "Compared to the most sophisticated computer that we have in the world, the mind is superior ten to the fifty-ninth power. If it were only ten times as effective as the computer, that might be understandable; ten followed by fifty-nine zeroes is hard to imagine."

Recently I read in an educational journal that the internal connections of the brain are conservatively estimated to ten followed by 5.6 million miles of zeros.

Who knows? All we really know is that there is tremendous power that can work for us when we let our minds get turned in the right direction. And there is tremendous destructive power when we let our minds get turned in the wrong direction.

Who turns the mind on? Who is the true helmsman? If I want creative thoughts, I have discovered, I need to turn to the Creator. The Scriptures are full of insights. James, the brother of Jesus, wrote a small volume that bears his name. It, I knew, was filled with practical suggestions for positive living.

I asked myself the question, Who really controls us? James comes up with an amazing answer: Words control the world.

Even more amazing, the spoken word has unbelievable power. Not only does it have power to change the people who hear the words; it has even more power to change the people who speak them. Listen to this:

> If any man offend not in word,
>> The same is a perfect man,
>>> And able also to bridle the whole body.
> Behold, we put bits in the horses' mouths
>> That they may obey us;
>>> And we turn about their whole body.
> Behold also the ships,

Which though they be go great,
    And are driven of fierce winds,
Yet they are turned about with a very small helm,
    Whithersoever the governor listeth.
Even so the tongue is a little member,
    And boasteth great things.
Behold, how great a matter a little fire kindleth.
And the tongue is a fire, a world of iniquity:

So is the tongue among our members,
    That it defileth the whole body,
        And setteth on fire the course of nature;
            And it is set on fire of hell.
For every kind of beast, and of birds, and of serpents,
    And the things in the sea,
        Is tamed, and hath been tamed of mankind:
But the tongue can no man tame;
    It is an unruly evil, full of deadly poison.
Therewith bless we God, even the Father,
    And therewith curse we men,
        Which are made in the similitude of God.
Out of the same mouth proceedeth blessing and cursing.
    My brethren, these things ought not so to be.
Doth a fountain send forth at the same place
    Sweet water and bitter?

                                    —James 3:2-17

What a powerful thing the mind is. Every atom of our body responds to what our mind thinks. When the mind thinks happy thoughts, a smile emerges. When the mind is filled with worry, anxiety, or bitterness, the digestive juices slow down. Pain and sickness may come.

These are simple illustrations. There are doctors who feel that even cancer may have its roots in the stressful state of mind.

The Greeks had two words, *psyche* (mind) and *soma* (body), that they felt were closely related. This is not a new idea. Doctor Maxwell Malz's book *Psycho-Cybernetics* develops this concept in detail.

The big question still must be answered. What triggers the activity of the mind? How do you control it? James, the brother of Jesus, gives the answer.

There really is a governor or helmsman of the mind. He is essentially the one who guides us to our destiny. Who is he? The tongue.

What we speak is what we are. What we speak we will become. Though I have read these words of James many times, they still frighten me with their statement: "[The tongue] defileth the whole body, and setteth on fire the course of nature."

Not only are the things within us affected by what we speak, but unbelievable as it sounds, the things around us are affected by what we speak. James's words hint at ideas that are so far reaching that we cannot overestimate their power.

Do you have a friend who was told as a child, "Your nose is too big" or "You are such a clumsy child"? Have you observed that a few words often spoken in wrath or frustration can change the destiny of a child? A child can with words like these be locked in a prison of self-rejection. Words that vibrate in the air for a few seconds can reverberate in a life as long as it lasts.

Have you noticed how often your own life is controlled by the words of another? A compliment may nourish your spirit for days—maybe a lifetime.

Words spoken to us change us. But what about words spoken by us? They have even more power. They become the helmsmen of our life. What we talk about we become.

Jesus himself talked about this: "Every idle word they shall speak, they shall give account thereof. . . . For by thy words thou shalt be justified, and by thy words thou shalt be condemned" (Matt. 12:36-37).

Words are important for two reasons. First, words betray what we are. The Scripture says, "Out of the abundance of the heart the mouth speaketh." Then words determine what we will become. Words spoken casually, whether they are positive or negative, blessing words or cursing words, become self-fulfilling prophecy.

The more we talk about our troubles, the more troubles we will have to talk about. To talk about our troubles is like fertilizing weeds.

The more we speak of blessing, the more we seek to bless, and the more blessings we have. We may even shower blessings on people. Those who deserve blessings the least need them the most.

Jesus said, "Bless them that curse you, do good to them that hate you, and pray for them which despitefully use you, and persecute you; that ye may be children of your Father which is in heaven" (Matt. 5:44-45).

Does this begin to sound like the Parallel Principle? When you act like God acts, you become godly, literally children of God. You inherit the celestial genes. God is a blesser. Those who share his nature also bless.

Chapter 10

A Few Thoughts about Winking in the Dark

Do you really have to say these things out loud? Isn't there just as much power in positive thinking?

Who would deny the power of a positive attitude? Dr. Norman Vincent Peale's immensely popular book, *The Power of Positive Thinking* continues to remind people of the tremendous power of positive thought.

There is even greater power in positive talking. Actually, the making of sounds creates miracles. If this is not so, why does James talk so much about the power of the tongue, as we saw in the last chapter? Why did he say the "tongue is a fire"?

Isn't it just as bad to think a thing as to say it? No. The tongue is the helmsman, the guiding force. The mind follows what the mouth speaks. It is not important whether anyone hears us or not. We hear. Our whole nature responds. The world around us (even though I cannot explain this) responds in an unbelievable way. Could we have hinted at this when we sang as children, "All nature sings and round me rings/The music of the spheres"?

To think of influencing the world of nature with words of

blessing may require more faith than you have at this moment. Put the whole idea aside. You will soon have even more creative thoughts than this.

Accept the concept of blessing merely because the Bible tells us to "bless the Lord . . . all his works in all places of his dominion." Accept the words of James: the tongue sets on fire the course of nature. Accept the stories of other people who have learned the power of blessing. Begin to bless—out loud.

Dr. Roy Lockwood repeated to me a proverb taken from the world of advertising people: "A man who does not advertise is like a man who winks at his girl friend in the dark. He knows what he is doing, but nobody else does."

That is true of advertising, Doctor Lockwood, but is not true of blessing. When you speak words of blessing whether anyone else hears them or not, you are affected by them. When you actually talk blessing you are disturbing the sound waves and you are starting a miracle. It is a miracle in you. And it is a miracle around you.

One day Ernie Gross and I were taking a walk from our hotel in Jerusalem to the Damascus Gate, the entrance to the fabulous old city. Our conversation was interrupted by the loud voices of children.

"What is all that?" Ernie asked.

"A school," I replied.

"The teacher must be out of the room for all the children to be talking at once," Ernie observed.

"Aha, my friend," I said, "you have the misfortune of thinking that school in this part of the world is like school in the United States. In the American school system under which you and I were trained, the role of the teacher is to talk and the role of the students is to sit still and listen.

"Ancient civilizations have learned a better way," I continued. "They encourage the students to recite out loud—to vocalize. Since kids are going to talk in class in spite of all you can do, why not encourage them to talk about the lesson."

During the next few hundred yards of walking I expounded the values of "out loud learning." First the eye has to see the words for the mind to comprehend them. That is the American way.

Here in Israel we are seeing all the other senses involved in learning. Not only must the mind receive the words, but the tongue has to speak them. Then the ear has to hear them. The tongue is a powerful educator.

Maybe Doctor Lockwood is right. To think a thing and not say it is like winking in the dark. You miss a lot.

A Word to the Timid

Do you feel funny when you talk to yourself? You shouldn't. It is one way of having an understanding audience.

Herb Thompson, who was raised in the rocky hills of eastern Kentucky, has a kind of independent thought that seems to thrive well in lonely places. He asked me, "Berk, do you ever talk to yourself?"

I admitted that I did, but that I felt a little ashamed of it.

"Don't feel bad about that," Herb said, "the Bible encourages it. David did it. And David was a man after God's own heart, a man stamped with the nature of heaven."

Herb continued, "Remember how Psalm 103 begins? It begins with David talking to his soul, as though his soul were sitting in a chair across the room from him.

" 'Good morning, soul, he would say. 'Today's assignment is for you to bless the Lord. And while I am talking to you, soul, I want to talk to all the rest of the class. Say these words, "All within me bless His holy name." '

" 'Then I want you to remember all the benefits we talked about yesterday. I am going to suggest a few to get you started . . . forgiveness and healing.' "

Herb continued talking to me. "Like any good school teacher, David finishes his assignment by summing it all up in one final word, 'Bless the Lord, O my soul.' "

"If you don't tell your soul how to act," Herb went on, "someone else will."

That helped me. I had always talked to myself, but I felt bad about it. In fact, I do more of it now. And I feel good about it. I even listen more.

You need to do this. If you feel self-conscious, go out in

the woods where no one but the woodpeckers will hear you. If the only forests near you are in the pages of the *National Geographic* magazine, learn to sing out loud while you work. In our society, singing at work is the sign of a happy mind; talking out loud is somewhat suspect.

A word of caution. Don't worry if your singing voice sounds, as Everett Minkler used to say, "like a ukulele in a cement mixer." Sing anyway. As I recall, the Bible encourages us to make a joyful noise and to sing to ourselves, making melody in our hearts. There doesn't seem to be much emphasis on our making a career out of it.

For most of us this is a good thing. Singing gives us a chance to ventilate our feelings, to say out loud the things that are in our heart.

Do it. Drive along the road and repeat the words of this magic psalm, "Bless the Lord, O my soul."

The first thing in the morning when you face the mirror that reflects the sleepy-eyed presence of a would-be blesser, smile and say, "Bless the Lord, O my soul. All that is within me, bless his holy name."

When these words have become a part of your normal way of talking, you will then learn how to bless others.

Try to imagine your life as a ship, maybe even a yacht. You are the owner. Your tongue, your power of speech, is the helmsman. Today you will put your will to work. You will instruct your life.

Give the orders aloud and clear: "Today, helmsman, you will bless the Lord. And today you will bless yourself. And today you will bless others."

Your words can take your ship of life to happy, sunlit harbors or head it into violent storms and treacherous rocks. You decide.

Blessing Your Enemies

There is no doubt about it. Jesus said to "bless your enemies." This is about as plain as words can make it. "Do not curse them; bless them."

As I write these words I am being "blessed" by a delightful

young couple in North Carolina. Don and Maxine McCall heard my lectures several years ago, began to listen to the recordings of them, and then searched to find exciting ways of proving the Parallel Principle. Since they know that I am finally putting these ideas on paper and am going to give them a wider audience, they have assured me that each day they bless me and my typewriter.

A year or so after they had heard these lectures, they spent an hour recounting the ways they had tested the concepts. Maxine is in the world of education and Don in the world of marketing. Both face pressures of all kinds. Then, together, they accept challenges of people who need redeeming but who seem to be outside the whole world of conventional religious helps.

Blessing works. It worked on an irascible teacher to whom they couldn't even talk. It worked on a young lady who was so captured by drug addiction that any attempt to help was met with vehement rejection.

It worked in business deals. There are times I think they ought to be writing this book instead of me. What is even better than all the answers that they have brought to others, is the fact that they have been blessed in scores of ways.

Blessing friends and enemies is a rewarding life-style. Do you have any enemies? Could you be one?

A particular comic strip has an interesting insight into a biblical truth. Says Pogo, "We has met the enemy and the enemy is us." Put in a little more acceptable grammatical form, St. Paul says, "[God] is able to do exceeding abundantly above all that we ask or think, *according* to the power that worketh in us" (Eph. 3:20).

Kelly Mitchell was as bright a child as we had in our school. But her mother tells of her early childhood when she still had a few things to learn.

Grandpa Sebastian came down from Ohio to see the family and while three-year-old Kelly sat on his lap he said, "Kelly, bring me your piggy bank."

When Kelly returned with her bank, he gave her a fifty-cent piece. "Put this in your bank," grandpa said.

She tried but it wouldn't go in. "Give me a dime," she said.

"A dime is not as much as fifty cents," replied her grandfather.

Reasoning would not work. Finally, in order to make his grandchild happy—and what grandparent does not make that a priority—Grandpa Sebasian gave Kelly a dime, which she happily deposited in her bank.

I smile at this. I smile, that is, until I realize that God's ability to give us unlimited blessings is limited by our ability to open up. Our slot is too small. If I cannot bless myself, I reject (certainly without wanting to or even knowing it) all the good things God is trying to offer.

How can we be our own worst enemy? Here is a dangerous intersection. Don't crash. When you discover that you have been by your negative attitude rejecting blessings, don't start saying mean things about yourself. That just complicates things. Don't be down on yourself because you have been down on yourself. After all, the future is ahead. You are a part of all the good things that happen. Bless God and bless yourself for the mistakes you have made. If you hadn't made them, you might never have looked for the road of blessing.

Chapter 11

A Beginner's Manual of Self-Blessing

Where do you start? It really doesn't matter where you start—just start somewhere. It is a lot like an auction. The bids can start anywhere with the smallest amount you are willing to invest.

Maybe the most obvious place to start is by looking at yourself and thinking of the things about which you complain the most. Why not start with your aches and pains?

Agnes Sanford, an Episcopalian minister's wife, has written a fascinating book titled *Healing Light*. She tells of a visit to a sick friend. She entered the hospital room with a cheery "good morning." Then she added, "How are you?"

"Terrible, my legs are killing me," the friend replied.

"Have you ever tried blessing your legs, talking nice to them?" Mrs. Sanford suggested.

"For heaven's sake, why should I?" the friend asked. "These legs are killing me. I am scheduled for an operation for varicose veins. Besides all the expense of surgery, there will be a long time of recovery. If it weren't for these miserable legs I wouldn't be in the hospital at all."

"How long have you had these legs?" inquired Mrs. Sanford.

"That is a silly question. I have had them all my life," her friend replied.

"And how long is that?" Mrs. Sanford asked.

The friend admitted, "Just between us girls, forty years."

"Do you mean that you have had these same legs for forty years and all this time they have worked for you without so much as a 'thank you'?" Mrs. Sanford replied.

"No, I guess not," said her friend.

"Well," continued Mrs. Sanford, "think about it for a few minutes. When you were born, you were born with two legs. One day as a tiny baby you looked down and discovered your tiny pink toes. You may even have been able to reach them. That must have been a good feeling."

"It must have been," the friend commented.

"Why don't you tell your legs 'thank you' for this?" suggested Mrs. Sanford.

"Now?" came the reply.

"Why not?" Mrs. Sanford asked. "You have waited forty years."

"Thank you, legs," said the friend gratefully.

"Wonderful," interjected Mrs. Sanford. "Now think about all the other times your legs have been your friends. Remember how you learned to crawl, how much fun it was to get into the cupboards and pull out the pots and pans? Whose legs did you use to crawl across the kitchen floor?"

"Mine, of course," her friend replied.

"Tell them 'thank you,' " Mrs. Sanford suggested.

"Thank you, legs," Mrs. Sanford's friend said, reluctantly. "I'm sorry I'm so late in telling you this."

"You are doing great for a lady who is out of practice," Mrs. Sanford pointed out, "but don't stop now. Think of learning to walk, to ride a tricycle and then a bicycle. Think of jumping rope and walking in the snow. Think of running to the mailbox to get a letter from your sweetheart. Your two legs carried you to all those places."

Mrs. Sanford continued, "As you lie here in your hospital bed, why not think of all the happy times in your life? Instead of dreading the surgery for which you are scheduled, spend the time blessing your legs for the many years they have worked for you. Remember the details of those experiences. Think of the music that accompanied you as you walked down the aisle of the wedding chapel. If you never walked again, you should be thankful for the forty years your legs have carried you."

After a prayer Mrs. Sanford left the room.

A few days later she returned to the hospital room to find an excited and jubilant woman.

"I can't wait to tell you what happened!" her friend exclaimed.

"Please tell me," Mrs. Sanford said.

"After you left my room the other day," the friend went on, "I thought to myself, That is the strangest advice I have ever heard. But what can it hurt to try the things Mrs. Sanford suggested? So I began remembering all the happy times of my life. My two legs had carried me into them. After a while when I was sure no one could hear me, I began to speak my thanks out loud. 'Thank you, legs,' I said self-consciously.

"One day something happened. I felt a warm glow on my legs. It felt as though they were reflecting light. Then the glow faded. My legs were suddenly healed. I do not need surgery."

As I read this story from Mrs. Sanford's book, I was impressed—and I was troubled. In the years that have passed since that time, I have had countless experiences that have assured me that blessing works this way. Not always is there the physical sensation, but blessing works.

How I Learned to Bless My Pain

There is strange wisdom in the world of blessing. You bless things not because they deserve a blessing, but because they *need* a blessing. That doesn't apply altogether in the case of blessing God, because he both deserves and needs our blessing. He is worthy of our praise as well. For the rest of us, and for many things that we encounter, blessing is conferred because it is needed.

Here is my story.

The congregation I pastored in Daytona Beach, Florida, needed a new building but there were no funds available. So we started construction with big dreams and a willingness to work. Men and women, boys and girls worked with their hands to "anchor their dreams to earth with deeds." For a year these wonderful people spent Monday and Thursday nights and all day Saturday working with whatever skill they had to construct the giant new auditorium.

My only talent was availability. I ended up on the unskilled labor detail. One of my first jobs was to help tear down an old building in which the church kitchen was located.

On one of the work nights, Earl Welborn and I were carrying a refrigerator out of the kitchen. The concrete floor had been broken up with a jack hammer. Walking was hazardous.

I stepped into a hole. That was the wrong thing to do. Immediately the pain in my back told me how very, very wrong it was. Thoughtfully—and rather quickly—I dropped the refrigerator.

I could not straighten up. Pain, agonizing pain, shot through my body. There was no way I could keep this pain a secret. A small crowd gathered.

"We had better pray for the pastor," someone suggested. "He's hurt."

Such a suggestion was not uncommon in those days. Apart from our natural concern for injured people there was an even more practical reason for prayer. We needed all the help we could get.

After the group prayed for me they asked, "How do you feel? Better?"

That was true. I did feel good because I was surrounded by caring, praying people. I felt better because they had put my case in the hands of the Great Physician. I felt better. My back did not. It hurt just as much as it had before. I couldn't straighten up.

To have pretended I was healed would not have been difficult if my illness had been a headache. I could have smiled long enough to go find an aspirin. With the back problem, there was no pretence possible.

What could I do? I began to walk around blessing God. I thought of the words of Isaiah 53. I realized that Christ had personally experienced my pain, just as he had carried my sin. In fact, when Jesus was healing people during his earthly ministry, Matthew reflected on these words: "[Jesus] himself took our infirmities, and bare our sicknesses" (Matt. 8:17). I blessed the Lord because he had voluntarily carried the sins and sickness of all the people of all time. He did this not for his benefit. It was for ours.

Then I blessed the pain itself. Strange as it seems, I thanked God for the pain. Without it I would never have understood how Jesus felt. Of course, my pain was trivial compared with his, but my pain let me know more than I would have known had I simply read the word *pain*. As a typical Christian I could sing the songs and hear the words that talked about the cross on which Christ was crucified. But pain was still just a word. Now it became a fact.

For fifteen minutes or so I walked around like a willow bent over in a windstorm. I kept my mind tuned to blessing. At the end of fifteen minutes the pain left me. I was able to stand straight and resume work.

When I remember scores of friends who have spent months in traction in a hospital simply because they injured their backs by picking up small objects, I bless God all over again for my deliverance.

More important than this, I have been able to share this story with scores of people who have felt pain. Many of them have told me, "As I lay on a hospital bed in extreme pain, my first thought was to complain. Then I remembered your story. As soon as I began to bless the Lord because he carried my pain, the pain began to ease. As I kept on doing this, I felt a healing touch."

You Don't Have to Step in a Hole

You don't have to wait until you step in a hole to learn to bless. You can begin any time. Everything around you is a miracle. Bless it.

We may talk about your wonderful mind, but it is so complex and miraculous that we really ought to start with something else—anything, maybe even your heart, for example.

Every twenty-three seconds your heart pumps the thirteen pints of blood through your entire body. It is everywhere. You cannot stick the point of a pin in your skin without finding blood. Doctors tell us that there are sixty thousand miles of arteries, veins, venules and capillaries through which this blood must pass. Some of these are the size of your little finger and some are so tiny that they can allow only a single cell to pass. Sixty thousand miles—that is more than the distance around the world twice. A miracle within our body!

This kind of faithful service goes on twenty-four hours a day. Maybe it gets a little jumpy sometimes. It may even have a little pain. Bless it. It needs it.

What if you worked for an employer for forty years and you never received so much as a thank you? Would you complain? Would you quit?

Your heart hasn't. Bless it. Your heart has been blessing you all of your life. With every pounding of the pulse it is saying "bless you." Why not return the favor? Psychologists talk about a new way of controlling the functions of your body. It is called biofeedback. It is claimed that the mind can "talk to" every organ of the body and change its behavior. Apparently this system works.

Why don't you and I invent the term *blessing-feedback.*

Bless Your Skin

When a dermatologist friend asked me, "What is the largest organ of the body?" I responded, "Probably the liver."

"Wrong," he said. "It is the skin."

So I started thinking about the skin to see how much I knew about it and to see how I felt about it. I quickly discovered that, although I was covered with it, I didn't know much about it. I am certain that I must have talked about it, but I had never talked to it. I am not even sure that I had said anything nice about it to anyone else.

A trip down memory lane was painful. Acne and allergies, blackheads and blemishes, and (would you believe it) wrinkles and sags—these were the things that got my attention. I am sure I complained. What an ungrateful tenant I had been as I lived in this house of skin.

Skin is a miracle. It is an energy-efficient air conditioning system that does not pollute with either noise or contaminants. It is a sanitation system that never rattles the garbage cans. It is a silent army that protects that body from millions of invading germs. It is a medical corps healing the wounds inflicted by an abrasive world. It is not only rugged and resilient; it beautifully covers the thousands of miles of blood vessels and muscles of the body. Without it we would look like an anatomy chart in a biology classroom.

Thank God for skin—sags and all. Bless you, skin.

Bless Your Hair

When the phone in my office rang, I had no idea that I would be speaking to one of my closest friends. He lives a thousand miles from me. Because the call came during the "high rate" time of the day, I guessed that there must be something important on his mind.

"I've got good news," he began. "I have been listening to the cassette tapes of your blessing lectures and, do you know what—you are telling the truth about blessing and what it can do."

"That's good to know," I replied.

"Well," he continued, "I had a set of those tapes around the house and I got to thinking that I would like to hear your voice again, so I started listening to them. Would you believe that I learned something about myself—something I never would have guessed? I always thought that I was a positive-thinking person, but I discovered that I have been cursing my hair."

"Really?" I asked somewhat incredulously.

My friend went on. "Oh, I don't curse it by using bad words, you understand. I just talked mean to my hair."

"That's bad," I said. "If you talk mean to your wife she won't stay around; she'll leave you. It could happen to your hair."

"It did," he said. "One morning as I combed my hair I noticed that a lot of it had been falling out. I kept combing what was left. Then I discovered that I was talking to myself—and of course my hair is part of myself: 'I can't do a thing with this hair—why is it falling out?' "

Then my friend continued: "Suddenly I realized that I had formed some bad habits over the years. I complained about my hair, its texture, its manageability, and its changing color. Never once had I complimented it or said kind things to it. That is terrible. No wonder my hair was leaving me strand by strand. So I started blessing it, saying nice things to it."

"What happened?" I asked.

"My hair has started coming back again," he said, "and it is coming in curly."

What could I say? What did I need to say? Just, "Bless you, my friend. Keep it up."

When I finished this telephone conversation I leaned back in my chair and thought, "It sounds trivial to waste time talking about falling hair. Or is it? The Bible talks about the hairs of our head.

Strange as it seems, the Bible has something to say about our hair. For example, "The very hairs of your head are all numbered" (Matt. 10:30) and "There shall not an hair of your head perish" (Luke 21:18).

Do these scriptures mean anything? Obviously they talk about the intimate knowledge of God. He knows everything about his children. And he is concerned about the most trivial of things.

According to specialists, the average blonde has 110,000 hairs on his or her head. The average brunette has 100,000. The average redhead has 90,000. These are averages.

The Bible says that God is more accurate. He knows the number of hairs of every person. When Paul assured his fellow travelers of their safety he said that not one hair of their heads would be lost. Jesus used the same expression to tell us of his protection.

When my wife, Berny, returns from the beauty shop she often says, "The operator told me that I have the easiest hair to work with he has ever seen. Sometimes the customers talk to me and say 'what beautiful hair you have.' "

"What do you say to them?" I ask.

She replies, "I always say, 'I have been blessed with good hair.' "

Then Berny will say to me, "I guess I have formed the habit of blessing my hair and not knowing that I was doing it. I have noticed however, that people who talk mean about their hair always have trouble with it."

If it seems trivial to start a spiritual pilgrimage with such a small thing as a strand of hair, remember the Chinese proverb "A journey of a thousand miles must begin with a single step." A tiny step that starts you on the highway of blessing is a very important thing. Start.

There are good economic reasons for blessing your hair. Recently a friend of mine who deplored his balding head had a hair transplant. Apart from the discomfort involved there was a significant cost. His new "crowning glory" cost more than a month's wages. A hundred thousand hairs that do not need to be replaced have a market value of fifty thousand dollars. Bless them. If for no other reason, bless them simply because they have stayed with you. Who knows what would have happened if you had sincerely blessed them before they were gone.

If, as the Bible says, God has an accurate count of the hairs of your head, he knows how many thank yous are due—probably overdue. A hundred thousand thank yous would certainly get you in practice.

"Let Everything That Has Breath. . . ."

You are breathing. Do you know what is happening?

Naturally, when you breathe your lungs fill with air. The oxygen gets into your blood stream and your entire body is nourished. Four or five minutes without oxygen will permanently damage your brain.

The fact that you are reading these words and understanding them means that your brain has been nourished by oxygen since your birth. Your lungs have been faithful. Have you blessed them?

Perhaps it will help to visualize them, to picture them, so that you will understand how miraculous they are.

Your lungs are not just two balloon-like organs inside your body. They are delicately built with countless air sacs and sensitive membranes. If you could stretch these surfaces out to form one continuous surface, there would be seventy-five square yards of surface. Seventy-five square yards. That is tremendous. Seventy-five square yards of carpet would carpet three rooms fifteen feet wide by fifteen feet long. Think of it. What a miracle. What a blessing. Your lungs have blessed you. Why not bless them? Learn to breathe deep and with each breath bless the Lord.

No wonder the psalmist said, "Let everything that hath breath praise the Lord."

Bless Your Kidneys

What happens when your kidneys stop? You do, too. Your body can sustain many losses without being seriously impaired, but when your kidneys stop working death follows. How blessed you are if they work.

Not long ago I visited a family whose mother had a kidney malfunction; she had to be taken regularly to the university hospital to be put on the dialysis machine. Without this she would have died. Not only were these trips to the hospital time consuming and inconvenient, but the actual cost to the family was $6,500 dollars a year.

If your kidneys are working normally you have good cause to rejoice. You save not only many hours a week, but also at least $6,500 each year for doing what you cannot help doing.

Everything within me is a miracle. "[Let] all that is within me, bless his holy name" (Ps. 103:1).

Bless My Mind

The mind is a miracle. It starts working the moment you are born and never stops for a single moment, night or day, until you stand to make a speech in public.

The mind is a miracle indeed. Even when our mind is paralyzed with fear it reveals its complexity. Compared to the human mind the most sophisticated computer of today's scientific world is about as complicated as a clothespin. Scientists, trying to discover the limits of the human mind, conclude breathlessly, "It's infinite. It has no limits."

How often do you bless your mind? Why is it more normal for us to forget all the things our minds do for us while complaining about the few times it takes a coffee break.

Personally I have been blessed with a wonderful memory. When I am asked about the secret of my memory I simply say that I speak kindly to my mind. If in the middle of an important address I forget an illustration or a set of statistics, I don't panic. I simply smile and say to my mind, "Bless you, mind, you have worked so hard and done so well that you deserve a vacation. Come back to work when you feel better."

Not surprisingly, my mind treats me very well. If I am trying to recall a face or a name and nothing seems to surface I simply say to my mind, "Bless you, mind. You have this information stored somewhere and when you find time would you send it up to me? You have been a wonderful friend for all these years and I don't want to impose on you." My mind appreciates that, and very soon the name comes to my lips.

Even as I write these words my mind is spilling out the information and insights it has gathered in many lands and many times. What an incredible blessing it is.

If I were locked in a dungeon my mind would be the silver ship that transported me again to all the exotic places I have visited in my entire life. If I were never to read another word my mind would pull book after book from the library of my memory. If I never saw another face as long as I lived, my mind would fill my days with smiling faces out of the past.

Should it be difficult to bless a friend like this?

Chapter 12

Living the Blessing Life

L iving the blessing life is not simply recognizing the physical or intellectual miracles housed in your personality; you must accept and bless the entire self. If you do not believe that God made and loves you, how will you convince others that God loves them? If you cannot bless yourself, how can you bless them?

A few years ago I met an old college classmate of mine. Since our school days he has gone on to get a doctoral degree in clinical psychology. He is presently employed in a hospital where he works with emotionally disturbed people. I knew this man, George Cerbus, was the person I wanted to talk to.

"George," I said, "is it true that self-dislike is one of the most expensive emotions we can have?"

"Certainly," George said," When people are not happy with who they are they will create a world for themselves in which they feel comfortable. Since this is not a real world, but a world of fantasy, they become psychotic or sick. To get them back to the real world is terribly difficult because they didn't like it in the first place."

Ralph Waldo Emerson suggested a key for happy living. He called it self-reliance. This is not exactly the same thing as blessing yourself, but it is one rung on the ladder.

"Trust thyself," he wrote, "every heart vibrates to that iron string. . . . There comes a time in every man's education when he realizes that envy is ignorance and imitation is suicide. . . . We reject our own ideas precisely because they are our own. They come back to haunt us with a certain alienated majesty."

You are unique. There is no one like you. To strive to be anyone else is to destroy the person that you are. To accept yourself as a special gift from God is to take the first step to the life of blessing. It is not likely that you will joyfully share yourself with others if you cannot accept yourself for yourself. To deny that unique person that you are is to hurl disdain in the face of God.

Let me make up a story.

The time is four o'clock in the afternoon. Six-year-old Randy walks into the kitchen where his mother is busy preparing supper.

"Look what I made for you in school," says Randy, proudly displaying a brightly colored piece of paper.

"What is it?" his mother asks.

"It's a picture," Randy replies. "I made it today especially for you. Here is the tree; here is a house. The sun is shining in the sky."

"Is that the sun?" Randy's mother inquires. "It looks like a spider hanging from the ceiling."

"Are you going to hang my picture on the wall, mother?" the boy asks, expectantly.

"Of course not," the mother replies. "It doesn't match a thing in the room. Besides, there are prettier pictures than yours on the covers of magazines."

"But mother, this is different," pleads the little boy. "I made it especially for you and I wrote your name on it. I even wrote 'love from Randy' with a big red crayon."

"Well thank you, Randy," says the mother. "Just lay your picture up here on the counter and we will do something with it."

The busy mother continues to get supper ready. Suddenly she realizes that she has not emptied the coffee grounds from the percolator since breakfast. Hastily she dumps the coffee grounds onto the colored paper that her son Randy has given her and throws them in the garbage.

"But mother," sobs Randy, "I made this picture for you. I made it myself. I thought you would like it."

This is an imaginary story. I made it up totally. It is a sad story, but it is not true. Yet even as I write it I can feel the tears start in my eyes. Though I have written this story I really cannot imagine any mother acting as Randy's mother did. She would certainly have to have a bag of gravel for a heart.

Now, if we can become emotional about a piece of paper hastily covered with crayon marks by a six-year-old child, if we can lament the hardheartedness of a mother who scorns the creation of her child, what shall we say of our own self-rejection?

You are a creation of God. Whether you think of yourself as an accident of either your parents or mother nature, you are far from this. You were first conceived in the thoughts of the universe's greatest thinker. You are like no one else. You were designed individually, lovingly, and purposefully.

If, for whatever reasons of foolish comparison, you crumple your life like a piece of waste paper and hurl it in the world's rubbish heap, God must weep. If you curse yourself, how can you call that humility?

Sometimes in the confusion and disarray of new construction a building looks like a disaster area. But contractors who walk around the piles of rough timbers and disturbed earth keep blueprints in their hands. The growing pains do not trouble them. They bless each sign of progress because they know that a magnificent building will one day stand where today there is only confusion.

What a miracle you are. You are composed of countless atoms—millions of them could dance together on the head of a pin. Yet each of these tiny atoms remembers the gleam in its Creator's eye when he created it. It was made for a purpose—a glorious purpose.

There is no way to avoid the lesson. Bless yourself. You are not only made by God; you are loved by him.

Strange as it seems, our entire society appears to be bent on making us feel dissatisfied. People who are old are encouraged to think that youth is the only good time of life. Young people are led to believe that happiness can come only with mature years. Babies are hurried into the growing-up process and growing-up people are pressured into the slowing-up process. We are assured that it is better somewhere else.

If we are born in the country, we are led to believe that "it is too far from everything." If we are born in the city we are told that moving back to nature is the only way to live.

If we are forever dreaming of the person we ought to be or the place we cannot be, we never accept who we are and where we are. So we miss life.

It was a custom of Old Testament characters to erect a stone altar at various places and say, "Surely God is in *this* place." You are standing in a wonderful place for an altar. Why not build an altar of blessing for who you are and where you are?

God is blessing you. When you bless yourself, you think like God thinks. That's not a bad idea. Look what happens when God begins to think.

It's Hard to Splash out of an Empty Cup

We smile indulgently as we hear of the foolish spectator who asked the builder how he started construction on a home. "Do you start at the top and work down or do you start at the bottom and build up?"

We all know that we start with foundations. If you have followed the blessing path to this point, you know that all great things come from God. The "Doxology" has become more than a tip-of-the-hat to religious tradition. "Praise God from whom all blessings flow" sounds more like a scientific statement.

God is the source. He is the blesser. When we respond to him in blessing his name, something happens to us. Regardless of how imperfect we may be, or how imperfect our world may be, we can find no fault with God. We bless him.

When we do this, something happens to us. We are free to accept ourselves and to bless ourselves because God has blessed us and accepts us.

At first it seems almost selfish to bless ourselves before we try to be a blessing to other people, but this is the only way it will work.

Having taken the first two steps, we are ready to take the most enjoyable step of all. We learn to bless other people and even inanimate objects.

Tillie Was a Remarkable Car

In Montana a charming enthusiastic woman came to the blessing lectures. One day she told me about her experience.

"I have really enjoyed learning about Psalm 103 and the life of blessing," she said. "Actually I must have known some of these things all the time because I discovered that if you talk kindly to things they work better. So I have talked to my car and to my flowers. But I wouldn't tell anyone about it.

"I used to bless my car," she continued. "The more I talked to it the better it ran. Although the odometer registered more than 200,000 miles, it kept running without trouble. Since I am not the fix-it type, I sort of let the outside deteriorate. It began to look terribly shabby, but it still ran like a charm. I really didn't know what to do. I still liked the car but was getting ashamed to drive it.

111

"Tillie had been such a good friend to me that I didn't have the heart to sell her to a junk dealer, or someone who might not love her. So I decided on a way to have 'death with dignity.' I entered Tillie in a demolition derby. That way she could go out in a blaze of glory."

The story intrigued me. I could imagine that ancient Oldsmobile coughing her way to destruction. "What happened?" I asked.

She replied, "Would you believe that it lasted to the end of the race? When it finally came to a stop, the last car on the field, all the tires were still intact, the battery, hanging by a wire, was still working. The alternator was fastened by a single bolt, but it was still charging. If I were ever going to get rid of that car I would have to beat it to death with a stick. But how can you do that to a car you love?"

Blessing works—even on old cars.

This story brought back memories. When my own old automobile—to whom I always spoke kindly—registered 100,000 miles, my wife Berny and I had a little service of blessing for it. Even now when I add oil to the crankcase I tend to think of this as a kind of anointing.

Maybe cars are not your problem. People may be, but it really is exciting to learn to bless things, too. Let me tell you about one machine that almost ruined the morale of our office.

Barbara and the Ominous Cast-iron Hulk

As you read this book you will discover that I am involved in religious work. For many years I was pastor of a church and administrator of a school. Both of these are holy callings. Somehow I have the feeling that people in secular callings misunderstand the temptations that come to "men of the cloth," as we are sometimes called. Somehow I feel that outsiders think we spend most of our time in the chapel meditating and getting a celestial suntan from the light that shines through the stained-glass windows.

Not so. There are worlds of misprinting typewriters and crochety duplicating machines that reach out to grab us with inky fingers as we are on our way to a society tea party. Then there are addressing machines. These are the complicated, necessary, capricious inventions of the regions of darkness. At least ours was—that is until Barbara came.

We had a wonderful staff of workers. The formula was simple. If you weren't wonderful you didn't stay. Though we didn't plan it that way, each new recruit in the office was assigned to the test-your-sanctification-on-the-addressing-machine department.

While I am about as mechanically inclined as a left-handed jelly fish, I was often called to fix the balking machine. I also had to calm the nerves of the frustrated operator.

"Do you talk kindly to the addressing machine?" I would ask.

Usually the answer was, "Well I didn't say anything bad, but I thought about it."

Then Barbara came. Barbara was assigned to the hulking gray machine.

"What does it do?" she asked innocently.

Trying not to act too critical, one of the senior secretaries said, "This machine puts addresses on envelopes automatically."

"Wonderful," said Barbara. "That seems so much more

efficient than doing it by hand. I can hardly wait to learn to operate it."

Nobody smiled. They figured Barbara would learn quickly enough. They let her.

No complaints came from the addressing department. Work came out in profusion and deadlines were met. I was never called to make emergency repairs. Finally I could stand it no more. I had to pay a visit to the addressing department. Barbara was operating the machine and instead of its normal bad habits, the gray hulk was singing like a stage-struck canary. Was Barbara a better mechanic than I?

I asked Nita, my secretary, about it.

"Barbara has a way with the addressing machine," she said. "She really likes it."

I began to miss my frequent visits to the addressing room. I felt unwanted, unneeded, a little like a parent losing his or her last child. So, with no excuse whatsoever I ventured out to see the formidable gray machine. As many fingernails as it broke and as many foreheads as it furrowed, I could not forget it.

The gray monster was still there, but it looked strangely different. I can't say that it looked modern—it looked like a prissy old lady wearing a benign smile. As a matter of fact, Barbara had put some pink plastic petunias on the machine.

"Barbara, what is your secret for keeping this machine running so well. Are you a natural-born mechanic?"

"I talk kindly to it," she said.

"Barbara, have you ever heard about blessing things?" I asked.

"No," she replied, "but I have heard that you give lectures about it. I'd like to hear them sometimes."

"Later," I said. "I don't want to confuse you with a lot of new ideas. Your system of blessing works quite well now."

Chapter 13

Bless the Kawasakis and the Hondas

Our home in Florida was located on a busy street. Since it was a large older-type home, we could not afford to air condition it, and so during the summer we slept with the windows open. This arrangement let in not only the breeze but the sounds of screeching tires and roaring engines.

One night this noise irritated me greatly. I had retired early because I had to catch an early plane the next morning. The more I tried to go to sleep the more the noises bothered me. Finally I tried to pray about this irritation. Nothing happened.

Somehow God spoke to my turning and tossing mind. He said, "Berquist, why are you so worried about getting to sleep?"

"I have to get up early to take a plane," I replied. "I have to fly clear across the country tomorrow."

"What are you going to do clear across the country that is so important?" God asked.

Taking my excuse further, I said, "I am giving my lectures on blessing—the ones on Psalm 103."

Then God said, "Did it ever occur to you to practice what you preach?"

"Sometimes," I replied. "Why?"

God said, "Do you realize that you have been lying here 'cursing' all the noises and the people who make them? Why don't you try blessing them?"

Since I was awake anyway, the idea didn't seem too bad. I tried to turn the stream of my thoughts from the negative to the positive, from cursing to blessing. I tried to imagine the thrill a teen-ager might have as he "varoomed" his Kawasaki under my window. "Bless you, son, and may God protect you tonight," I said softly.

As giant transport vans approached the stoplight, I tried to think of the loads of furniture they were carrying and the people for whom they were carrying them. People who are moving need my blessing. "Bless you," I said. "Driver, may you stay awake as you travel. May your cargo arrive safely with nothing broken but the monstrous vase that the people didn't know what to do with anyway."

The whole thing became a game. Just as I was getting to enjoy it, I fell into blessed sleep.

Jesus said, "Bless them that curse you."

A schoolteacher recently handed me an article from a newspaper whose name I didn't recognize. She asked me to read it and then to tell her what I thought of it.

I read it not once but twice. Both times there were tears in my eyes as I read the sensitive and caring words, words that had to have come from a loving person.

"Whoever wrote this must be a loving person," I said.

She smiled. "He is our 'blessing man.' "

"You mean he goes around blessing people?" I asked.

"Not quite," she replied. "He is a teacher I had to work with, a volatile man who was so hostile that no one could approach him. Those who could, avoided him totally. I couldn't—I had to work with him. I had to see him several times a day."

"What did you do?" I asked.

"About this time," she said, "my husband and I were listening to the lectures on blessing and we decided to see if that principle would really work. We started saying, 'bless you,' whenever we thought of him."

She continued, "Things began to change. Over a period of time he became the loving and caring person who could write what you have just read."

This is one of the laws of blessing. The less people deserve blessing the more they need it. People who bless nondeserving people receive the greatest blessing in return.

Someone once said, "Anger is a poison more hurtful to the cup that carried it than to the object on which it is poured." That is true—and sad.

It is also true that blessing sweetens the cup out of which it is poured at least as much as the objects on which it is poured.

Blessing and the Law of Increasing Returns

Looking back on the whole story of blessing, I find scores of illustrations. None is more powerful than the parallel wires. When the secondary wire gets in perfect alignment with the overhead wire, it becomes activated. Whether or not we understand the electronic principle, we can prove the principle at the human level any time we want to.

Just as God is merciful to those who don't deserve mercy (and that is the reason it is called mercy), we are asked to be merciful. Just as God blesses people according to their need and not according to their worthiness, we are asked to bless people. There is great reward for this obedience.

As soon as we start acting like God—not trying to be God—God's energy comes to us. As we start blessing other people, God's blessings come to us.

Charles Schwartz proved this. Charles is more commonly known as "Flop" to his friends in the small mountain town in Virginia. Saltville is my wife's home town, too. That is how I found Saltville.

I was invited to give my blessing lectures to the congregation in Saltville. As I described the Parallel Principle, Flop was an eager listener. One night he told me his story.

Flop was exposed to mercury as he worked in the chemical plant and became critically ill with mercury poisoning. For twenty-three days he lingered between life and death in the intensive care unit of Duke University Hospital. Doctors had exhausted every possible way of helping him. All he could do was to lie in pain and pray.

"One day as I lay on my bed praying," he said, "I felt terribly discouraged. Everything seemed hopeless. Finally I thought of a prayer I could pray. 'Lord I don't know how to pray; will you teach me?' "

Suddenly Flop felt an inspiration to pray for the other patients in the intensive care unit. "If I could not get help for myself," he said, "at least I may do something for them."

Flop continued, "Though I had no idea what was wrong with these people and although there was no way to explain to them what I was doing, I started blessing them.

"Miraculously I began to recover. Within one day I was so improved that I was transferred to a conventional hospital room. In three or four days I was allowed to go home."

This is the positive reward for blessing others. Returning to the ideas that are discussed in detail in the first part of this book, we discover that everything attracts to itself things like itself. Lives that are tuned to giving blessings receive blessings.

As I write these words I am in a lonely motel room with a noisy air conditioner doing its best to keep me company. Near me lies the morning paper with its screaming headlines telling of trouble all over the world. The inside pages continue the story of divorce and separations. We all want our share—and we want it first.

What would happen if people would adopt the Flop Schwartz Initiative Technique? We could pray, "I don't understand why the blessings I need don't come to me, Lord. But in the meantime there are a lot of people who need a blessing. Bless them."

The chemistry of the world would change. If only one person did this, things would change. I have seen it happen.

The Worst Story I Ever Heard

Well-known pastor and evangelist Dr. Dale Oldham claims that a sermon is just an excuse to string stories together. This doesn't seem far from the truth when you remember that Jesus, master teacher of all time, used stories to illustrate eternal truth.

Ross Minkler, a minister friend of mine, is a man of stories. He told me the worst story I ever heard. I am tempted to tell you that it is not true, but I am not sure myself. I will simply tell it to you and let you decide.

"Once upon a time," says Ross Minkler, "there were two brothers. As it happened, the younger brother was always successful in whatever he tried to do. Apparently all the family good luck had come to him, because the older brother was always a failure. If the older brother bought a car it turned out to be a 'lemon.' If the younger brother bought a car it turned out to be a classic, worth many times what he had paid for it. Stocks were the same way. The older brother's purchases always decreased in value and the younger brother's portfolio always skyrocketed. It was always that way.

"One day the older brother complained to God about the unfairness of it all. 'Surely,' he said, 'surely there must be a time in my life when I will be able to get some good things.'

"As he prayed an angel entered the room, saying, 'Your prayers have been heard. You will get whatever you wish.'

" 'Wonderful,' said the brother, 'but what is the catch to all this?'

" 'There are no "catches," as you call them,' said the angel. 'There is one condition. Whatever you get, your brother will receive twice as much. You will have one hour to consider what you want to ask for.'

" 'I don't need an hour,' the brother said. 'I don't need five minutes. I know what I want now—I want to have one of my eyes put out.' "

As Ross told me this story I asked myself, Can it be true?

At first I thought it was impossible. God would not allow anyone to imprison himself or herself in his or her own hostility and selfishness. But he does.

Then I thought of the stupidity of the human mind. Would anyone begrudge his or her fellow humans a blessing simply because he or she was covetous? But we do. When we withhold from others, we rob ourselves.

Your Blessing Potential

Imagine you are greeted by an angel tomorrow morning. His first words are, "Here is a one-hundred-dollar bill. There

is only one condition to your accepting it. You must give it away by midnight."

Can you imagine what you would think? Who is worthy of such a gift? Who deserves it? So all day long you finger the bill. Mentally you list people to whom you might give the bill. Then you cross them off. They are not quite deserving. At last the day is almost over and you realize that you must give the one hundred dollars to someone whether that person deserves it or not. The day has been a long one filled with indecision.

Oh well, you decide, I had better give it to the first person I meet whether he or she deserves it or not. Grudgingly you hand the wrinkled currency to a stranger.

Reaching into your pocket to affirm its emptiness, you discover a miracle. There are two one-hundred-dollar bills in your pocket. Your giving has multiplied money. Perhaps it would be safe to risk one of these again. You do and the multiplication continues. For the one you gave you have two more. Soon you are stopping people on the street to bless them with your generosity. Why didn't I start sooner? you think. Blessing is like that. It works on the law of increasing returns.

Dan and Donna Archibald live in Montana where Dan farms a large tract of ranch land. All his life Dan has worked hard—maybe too hard. Last summer he heard the blessing lectures and decided to experiment on his own. He began to bless his farm, his neighbors' farms, and even his children.

Recently I visited Dan's farm and he pointed out his "blessing road." Along this mile of dirt road Dan has found a place to walk while he repeats Psalm 103 and blesses the lands all around him.

"Strange as it sounds," he told me, "rains didn't come to our state this year as they should have. But they did come to my farm and those bordering on mine. I blessed them, and I blessed God for them. How can you lose on a deal like that?"

Lowell Wilson, with whom I have shared many hours,

ideas, and miles, once said to me, "I don't remember asking God for anything during recent years. I simply kneel and say to him again and again, 'Bless the Lord, O My soul: and all that is within me, bless his holy name. Bless the Lord, O my soul, and forget not all his benefits.' " Perhaps this is the finest kind of prayer.

There is no end to the story I am telling you. If some of the stories I have told seem almost magic, let them seem so. You do not have to believe them. All you have to do is to realize that there are two powerful forces in the world: blessing and cursing. Decide to line up with the power of blessing and you will have stories enough for a book of your own. If you write it, I have a title: *How I Became a New Person through the Power of Blessing*.

CHRISTIAN HERALD ASSOCIATION AND ITS MINISTRIES

CHRISTIAN HERALD ASSOCIATION, founded in 1878, publishes The Christian Herald Magazine, one of the leading interdenominational religious monthlies in America. Through its wide circulation, it brings inspiring articles and the latest news of religious developments to many families. From the magazine's pages came the initiative for CHRISTIAN HERALD CHILDREN'S HOME and THE BOWERY MISSION, two individually supported not-for-profit corporations.

CHRISTIAN HERALD CHILDREN'S HOME, established in 1894, is the name for a unique and dynamic ministry to disadvantaged children, offering hope and opportunities which would not otherwise be available for reasons of poverty and neglect. The goal is to develop each child's potential and to demonstrate Christian compassion and understanding to children in need.

Mont Lawn is a permanent camp located in Bushkill, Pennsylvania. It is the focal point of a ministry which provides a healthful "vacation with a purpose" to children who without it would be confined to the streets of the city. Up to 1000 children between the ages of 7 and 11 come to Mont Lawn each year.

Christian Herald Children's Home maintains year-round contact with children by means of an *In-City Youth Ministry.* Central to its philosophy is the belief that only through sustained relationships and demonstrated concern can individual lives be truly enriched. Special emphasis is on individual guidance, spiritual and family counseling and tutoring. This follow-up ministry to inner-city children culminates for many in financial assistance toward higher education and career counseling.

THE BOWERY MISSION, located at 227 Bowery, New York City, has since 1879 been reaching out to the lost men on the Bowery, offering them what could be their last chance to rebuild their lives. Every man is fed, clothed and ministered to. Countless numbers have entered the 90-day residential rehabilitation program at the Bowery Mission. A concentrated ministry of counseling, medical care, nutrition therapy, Bible study and Gospel services awakens a man to spiritual renewal within himself.

These ministries are supported solely by the voluntary contributions of individuals and by legacies and bequests. Contributions are tax deductible. Checks should be made out either to CHRISTIAN HERALD CHILDREN'S HOME or to THE BOWERY MISSION.

Administrative Office: 40 Overlook Drive, Chappaqua, New York 10514
Telephone: (914) 769-9000